SHOW NO FEAR
Redux

Bill Carson
2014

Copyright Bill Carson 2014

All rights reserved

No part of this book may be reproduced in any form by photocopying or by any electronic or mechanical means, including information storage and retrieval systems, without permission in writing from the copyright owner of this book. Short extracts of up to 100 words may be used in book reviews.

www.billcarsonbooks.com

Edited and proofread by www.edit-my-book.com

Cover design www.cafepixel.co.uk

Layout www.polgarusstudio.com

They say, best men are moulded out of faults, and, for the most, become much more the better for being a little bad.

William Shakespeare

CONTENTS

Prologue: Ancient Guardians vii
Introduction xv
Chapter 1 – Young Warrior 1
Chapter 2 – Fighting Fit 11
Chapter 3 – First Night Nerves 18
Chapter 4 – The Sloane Rangers 23
Chapter 5 – The Professionals 29
Chapter 6 – Street Fighting Man 39
Chapter 7 – Chav Town 45
Chapter 8 – My Manor 48
Chapter 9 – The Knife Man Cometh 63
Chapter 10 – The Fairer Sex 75
Chapter 11 – Reality 86
Chapter 12 – Stand Your Ground 91
Chapter 13 – A Descent Into Violence 96
Chapter 14 – Strange Days 112
Chapter 15 – End Game 125
Epilogue 132
Author bio 135
Glossary of Slang 137
Gallery 139

Prologue: Ancient Guardians

The history and origins of bouncers – or gatekeepers as they were known in ancient times – goes way back. It's not the oldest profession but it is certainly one of them. Through my research I have found that we can trace this occupation back to before the Ancient Greeks, and guardians of doorways are even mentioned in the Old Testament. The duties of the 'ancient guardians' were to protect the treasures of the many temples from theft and to eject any undesirables; these gate/doorkeepers were used as a visible threat to any would-be troublemakers.

The importance of the doorman as a person allowing or not allowing entry is found in a number of plays and stories throughout the centuries. There is even a mention that doormen were said to be used as guardians to the gates of the underworld in one Greek myth, and in Roman times noble and less noble households employed an ostiarius, which translates as 'doorkeeper'. These ostiarii were employed to guard the entrances of the wealthy houses, temples and dens of iniquity and had the power to eject troublemakers.

In the Old Testament, the Levitical temple had a number of doorkeepers on duty to keep individuals out of the sacred areas and to deter thieves. Another allusion to a man guarding a doorway is in a play called *Bacchides* which was written in about 200 BC by the Roman playwright Titus Maccius Plautus. He writes of a large and powerful individual being used as a threat to get an unwanted visitor to leave.

So if we quickly push forward the lever on our time machine and zoom to the nineteenth century, we find that the function of the bouncer is still pretty much the same and the modus operandi hasn't changed for a couple of thousand years. Like their ancient counterparts, they were still being recruited from the lower elements of society. Ex-cons, gunfighters, pugilists, prize fighters, gamblers and bar room brawlers, which of course all makes perfect sense: who else would be best equipped to deal with the murderers, thieves and violent drunken men but their own kind? And the tougher they were, the better.

In the Wild West of the 1880s, for example, bouncers were primarily employed to look after the saloons and brothels and the girls who worked in them. The prostitutes in turn saw themselves as a higher class of sex worker and were therefore able to charge a slightly higher rate due to their salubrious surroundings and their 'minders', who guaranteed that the patrons paid up.

***

If we now move on to the 1920s and 30s, many bouncers were associated with and were recruited from organised crime gangs. Some notorious gangsters started their careers as bouncers. Al 'scar face' Capone, possibly the most famous/infamous of them all, was a bouncer in his early days. It was while working as a bouncer that he acquired two scars on his face after an altercation with a punter. During the prohibition years in America, bouncers were employed to protect the assets at the illegal speakeasies and underground gin joints.

We will now shoot forward to England during the 1960s and 70s and take a look at London specifically. Most of the bouncers back then were still mainly ensconced within the shady realm of the underworld and hired by real gangsters, and so a certain type of person was sourced. When they were not robbing trains or banks and killing each other, they were employed as bouncers at the clubs which were owned and run by the underworld.

The Kray twins and the Richardson brothers, for example, ran the whole of London at that time. London was basically like a big cake sliced in two and it stayed that way for many years. Back then there was much rivalry and the guys working on the doors always felt that it was necessary to carry or have an 'equalizer'. This would usually take the form of a clumping tool of some description, and there was always a prerequisite to have a firearm readily to hand, which would be hidden in some discreet cupboard or behind a curtain somewhere close to the door.

***

I took up this somewhat ignoble profession back in the early 1990s. At first it was purely out of necessity in order to gain a little extra cash, but I kind of got sucked into it and stayed for longer than I should have done. Many of my colleagues at that time seemed to be recruited from the ranks of ex-boxers, ex-cons, martial artists or just your good old fashioned bog standard street fighters.

When I worked on the doors, I always stood up to be counted. My brethren and I adopted a zero tolerance attitude which would often get us into difficulties with the fraternity of the local hard men. We would inevitably fall foul of them and be forced into fist fights to implement our policies and get our message across.

Sometimes I was on my own out there and with nothing or no one else to count on. I would often feel incredibly vulnerable, and to know that you had a serious backup plan was reassuring and, to me, entirely necessary. It is total fantasy to believe otherwise and many bouncers at one time or another carried something with them in case of attack to even up the odds. However, many bouncers that I have encountered carried weapons with them out of the fear of retribution, which is totally logical. Without a shadow of a doubt, you will acquire a few enemies in this game. It was all just part and parcel of the shady world of the unlicensed tough guy bouncer of yesteryear.

In the way that I approached this occupation I would, by today's standards, be branded as old school. My way of acting or thinking would not be permitted in any way shape or form and would be totally alien in the modern era.

Today things have changed and it's different out there. The bouncer/door-host/door supervisor/security operative in the modern era is now licensed. The industry has been sanitised and cleansed of the mind-set and image of the big, burly, shaven-headed, scar-faced, broken-nosed, cauliflower-eared, knuckle-dragging, troglodytic Cro-Magnon type. And in doing so, the deterrent factor has now been greatly diminished.

Today we have a new breed of young, fresh-faced men and women who are all indoctrinated with the meek and mild mannered approach. They are taught how to counter aggression by using passive conflict management techniques, and by law they are required to display their real names on ID cards on arm bands for all to see. When I worked the doors, our identities were always a closely-guarded secret. My compatriots and I permanently worked under pseudonyms for reasons of 'self-protection', which ultimately was the name of the game back then.

However, from what I see on TV and read in the newspapers the job is just as dangerous as it ever was. Compared to the past, it is probably more challenging due to the restrictions that are now in place. In my day you had a good chance of getting away with clumping your way out of trouble, which I quite often had to do.

For those of you who choose to work the doors today, I, for one, salute you. I say that simply because if you have not done this job, you have absolutely no idea of how problematic and tense it can get sometimes. And so if you are considering embarking on a career as a door supervisor, then know this: don't believe the hype about this type of work. It is not a glamorous or a praiseworthy profession, and nobody really gives a damn about you. You're on your own, except for the people that you are working with, but that's only because of its symbiotic relationship. They rely on you and vice versa. But sadly, as I have learned from personal experience, even they can let you down sometimes. When that happens it can all end with terrible consequences, as it did one night for a good friend of mine.

The way I did it was to treat people the way I would like to be treated myself: clichéd, you may say, but none the less true. I really did try and keep the scumbags away from the ordinary punter. If you think along those lines, you will not go far wrong. You can never allow yourself to switch off for a minute and let your guard down, assuming that the punters are as nice and as pleasant as you may think they are. The old saying, 'familiarity breeds contempt', is very fitting for this line of work. The truth is there are a lot of extremely nasty, psychotic, cowardly bastards out there. Some of them would think nothing of stabbing you or putting a bullet into you on the crazy premise of the often misused term 'disrespect'.

It was that great character and the king of the bouncers, the late Lenny Mclean, who once said: "Many doorman of today are just posers and they don't know how to rough up a punter."

Who am I to argue, and I know what he meant by it. The point is, bouncers are not able to do this nowadays as they would be arrested on the spot, and moreover the approach/tactics and indoctrination of the modern doorman are now completely different. The role has distanced itself from the ancient and the old school ways. And that is what makes the narrative you are about to read unique, as you will probably never read the like again.

SHOW NO FEAR REDUX

Introduction

It's been ten years now since *Show No Fear*, a bouncer's diary, was published and almost twenty years since I donned my righteous armour. So to mark this ten year anniversary, I have decided to revisit the old diary, dig out the original manuscript, add some much needed updates and re-release the book. I am now very happy with the end result and have created a very different book from the original.

Show No Fear is an account of how I became involved in the shady world of nightclubs and bouncers. The book grew out of a diary which I kept when working on the doors. I would jot down the incidents as they occurred. Nothing is exaggerated in this book – this is exactly how it was and how I felt at the time. This job was not glamorous in any way shape or form. This is not a glamorous industry, and so, having said that, this book may not be what some people expect.

Since I published *Show No Fear*, many other books on this subject have appeared. I've read a few: some are good, some are bad and some seem to have been written by total fantasists. So if you want to read a book about gunplay, extreme violence, blood 'n' guts, fast cars, psychopathic gangsters, death and mayhem, then I suggest you pay a visit to the crime fiction section.

However, there are scenes and moments of real violence here. You will also discover that a real fight is nothing like it is depicted in the movies. If you are a fan or a practitioner of the martial arts, boxing or unarmed combat, you will also find something of interest here.

This book is a little sad in places and you will meet a few strange, odd, violent and unpleasant characters. My aim is to try and put you, the reader, in my shoes so you can experience what it would be like to stand on the front door of a nightclub. You'll be right with me from my very first night to my last night.

So if you feel you are ready, then stiffen the sinews, summon up the blood, take a deep breath, strap on your bulletproof vest and come with me. Remember to show no fear as we meet the weirdos, drunks, bullies, dealers and hordes of weekend warriors face to face.

SHOW NO FEAR REDUX

By Bill Carson

Dedication

This book is dedicated to the memory of Johnnie Ennis (the Uncle), Jack Coleman (Crackerjack), Bill Smith (German), Reggie Brown (Brownie), Patrick Boyle (Jock), Andy Barker, Jim Brompton, Jim Parsons, Tony Palmart, Gretchen, John and Sylvia Bradley and Ben Harper. Be seeing you all at sundown.

~~~

CHAPTER ONE
YOUNG WARRIOR

I have always done some sort of training. I started with karate. It was the summer of 1973 when it all began and I must have been about fourteen at the time. The karate club was only a short walk from my house. The first I knew of the club's existence was when I saw a friend of mine walking through the park with his sports bag. I was playing football and I called out and asked him where he was going.

"I'm going to karate," he said.

Karate? That sounds interesting, I thought.

I fell into step with him and he explained that some fella had given him a good hiding. Revenge being his initial motivation, he'd decided to learn how to fight so that if he ever bumped into the guy again he could dispatch him with a few well-aimed karate chops on the back of the neck.

At the time, the TV series *Kung Fu* was being broadcast, and Bruce Lee and Chuck Norris fought their way across the cinema screens all over the world. These films were hugely popular and martial arts clubs were springing up all over the place in response to them. Even the singer Carl Douglas jumped on the band wagon with his single 'Kung Fu Fighting', which reached Number 1 the charts. Kids everywhere were making cat-like noises and hopping about and kicking each other up and down the playgrounds of England. The world had gone martial arts mad and Kung Fu crazy and, in doing so, had sowed the seeds for the future.

Some of the other lads decided to tag along with me as well. The building we arrived at was a large wooden construction with a corrugated iron roof. One half was a snooker club, the other a karate school. The two very different sports were divided by a thin wooden panelled wall. Once I was inside the club a sense of tranquillity descended over me: there was reverence here and I felt like it was supposed to be.

As we waited for the lesson to begin, we witnessed a few strange activities taking place. There were people bowing to each other and everyone was dressed in white pyjamas. They were doing some very odd limbering up exercises. As the instructor walked in, he bowed at the threshold and the students quickly and silently fell into line.

The other lads who came with me were all taking the piss and trying to act out the movements. Thankfully they left after a while. But I didn't: I stayed right to the end. I knew as soon as I set foot in the place that this was where I belonged. I joined up as soon as I could and I've never looked back. That was forty years ago and I have been involved in the martial arts ever since.

I didn't have a great deal of confidence when I was a kid. I was often thought of as a bit of a dreamer. I would run home if someone started picking on me. One reason that some people decide to run away instead of standing their ground to fight is through lack of knowledge. You don't know what to do when confronted with violence and so, as the adrenaline kicks in, you get scared and make a run for it. Karate made the difference for me, and from that moment on I stopped running. Karate gave me the knowledge to dispel my fears it also gave me the confidence that I thought I'd never have.

I stayed at the karate club for many years met and trained with some great people and I had some unforgettable superb times there. I can still remember the first real fight I had. I had a tough job in those days and was working as a scaffolder on a huge building site in central London with my dear old dad and all his mates. I think I was barely eighteen when I started working there. It was quite rough sometimes and I saw many fist fights occur. Generally they were quick and nasty little affairs, but having said that, they were all forgotten about the next day providing it was a fair fight. And sure enough, as day follows night, one afternoon it was my turn to provide the pugilistic entertainment.

I got along with most of the guys and was a popular lad, but there was one fella that I never liked who worked in a big labouring gang. He was a cocky and arrogant sort and he may well have thought the same about me. My old mate Martin and I were having a drink one lunch time in a pub around the corner from the building site when this fella walked in with a couple of his pals. They came straight over to us and gave us the type of stare that could only denote trouble. I didn't know what his problem was, and I never found out either.

Now I was weighing in at scarcely twelve stone back then, but my ace in the hole was the fact that I was strong and quick and also very good at the old karate. A stand-off ensued and a few words were exchanged and we eventually decided to take it outside. This was how we settled things in those days: man to man, a one on one straightener with honour.

We went outside the pub and stood toe to toe and squared off. Once the preliminaries were over we were both ready to do battle. As he made a move forward to deliver his attack, I smashed my shin bone into his thigh with everything I had in an all-or-nothing thigh kick. The force of it buckled his left leg and it bowed like a palm tree in a hurricane. He dropped to the ground, cracking both elbows and the back of his nut against the pavement. The gamble had paid off because he'd had enough, and the fight – if you can call it that – was over in seconds. The next day it was all forgotten about; it was something that was just accepted back in those days and you simply moved on.

For me, I have found that the build up to these types of altercations can be the most distressing part – much worse than the actual combat itself. It's the not knowing and the pondering on the unknown that gives you the hebejebes. You have to try and shut it out of your mind and get to it.

Fear is met by courage and destroyed.

Saturday mornings were without a doubt the best karate training session: we called it the animal hour. Only a select few used to turn up, which was good as that meant some close tuition. The lesson would always start in the same way and we would assemble in two lines, standing one directly behind the other.

"Take your Gi tops off front line, turn around and face the person behind," the instructor said. (The Gi training suit is worn by karate and judo practitioners.) He would then tell us to plant twenty hard punches into our partner's stomach and then he would return the compliment. The force of the blows would sometimes actually knock me backward into the wall. Once we'd completed the punching, we would be straight down pumping out press-ups, sit-ups and squats, and then we would go for a two-mile run through the streets in bare feet. That was the warm-up out of the way. When we came back from the run, we began practicing some rudimentary karate training which consisted of blocking routines and different striking and kicking methods. After that, the fun would really begin. This was the free sparring, my favourite part. The only protection we were wearing was a groin guard. There were no gloves and no gum shields.

I remember getting changed after one session, and when I took off my groin guard I saw that the plastic protective cup was completely smashed in two. Everything else was intact, thank God. That's what it was like. The next week I fractured someone's ribs with a reverse punch; you would come out of there with bruises all over you.

This was the real deal. There was no pissing about. It was tough karate training in the Japanese style, bordering on brutality, and I loved it.

There was this one guy whose name I can't remember but I nicknamed him Hiza (*hiza* being the Japanese word for the knee) as the only technique he seemed to possess with any accuracy was the knee strike. He would suddenly get in close and grab hold of you and start smashing you up with knee strikes. It was as if he'd superimposed a bull's eye over your knackers and then he would commit himself to a full three-minute assault on them. My defence was to step to the side and try to keep moving, and when I got the chance I would punch him unmercifully about the ribs every time he came in close.

The techniques we practised were mainly geared for the 'knock down' fighting, which was exactly as it sounds: the idea was to knock your opponent down with full contact blows to the body to win. The training was extremely arduous and was definitely some of the hardest training I have ever experienced. It is not easy turning your body into a dangerous weapon.

After a couple of years of this, I discovered that I no longer had the fear that had once ruled over me.

'Our doubts are traitors, and make us lose the good we often might win, by fearing to attempt.' William Shakespeare.

I had now forged my body and mind in the fires of adversity. I'd gone through all of the tough training and come out the other side a better person. It is, of course, entirely up to you how hard you want to train, but if you put nothing in you'll get nothing out. I trained with full commitment every time, even when I was injured. I broke my toes and fingers on numerous occasions, but injuries like that were common and they never stopped me from training. I'd just strap them up good and tight and get right to it. I even carried on fighting when someone had shattered some of my teeth with a powerful roundhouse kick.

At traditional Japanese karate schools, hand conditioning is something that is practised regularly as it is part of the curriculum. Some karate schools do very little of this and at others there is no place for it at all. Situated in the narrow gravel alleyway alongside our little karate club were three punching posts set into the ground. Attached to these wooden posts were thick straw punching pads called *makiwara*. The idea was that as you repeatedly slammed your knuckles into the pad, it would toughen the impact area of the fist.

If you wish to begin *makiwara* training, you will need to start off by developing the punching techniques first. Correct punching is not easy and it takes a while to be able to punch the *makiwara* with force and without injuring your wrists. It takes years and years of dedicated unending practice to perfect these karate strikes.

To toughen the knuckles further we also did press-ups on our knuckles on pieces of flat pinewood board. I used to practice on the punching post a great deal. I even put one up in my back garden, and I still have one today outside my little gym. This type of training is only found in the toughest of karate schools. In my school, for your first dan (black belt), for example, you had to have fifty consecutive three-minute fights.

It was full contact and no gloves were worn. Kicking to the groin wasn't allowed and neither was punching to the head. Thigh kicks were my speciality: they are powerful, painful kicks and if you deliver one in the right spot on your opponent, the fight will be over. I received a kick in the thigh in one match that was so hard the next day the mass of bruising came out on the opposite side of my leg. I was hobbling about like Long John Silver for a week.

Another knock down fight I remember was when I had been struck with a spinning back kick. The guy's heel had struck me with full power to the side of the head, which dropped me down onto one knee. I didn't feel any pain as such, but the room and my legs went a bit wobbly for a moment, and then I saw a group of perfectly formed five-pointed three-dimensional little golden stars spinning slowly in front of me. I used to think that was something that you only saw in cartoons. Take it from it me, it actually does happen. I got back up quite quickly, though, and continued to fight on. I was groggy but still managed to get in a few good blows. I had a massive headache afterwards and a black earhole for a couple of weeks.

You have to learn to take it before you can dish it out.

Every winter we were invited to take part in a Japanese-style training course which was held at a private school in Buckinghamshire. The school had vast grounds, where we would all be running around in the mud, rain and snow. Sparring matches were organised in the fields, where we also took part in the roughest game of British bulldog you have ever seen: flying kicks and elbow strikes were traded with equal enthusiasm.

But the best part of the course was saved until the end. In the grounds they had a huge waterfall, and each of us would to go under it to execute fifty karate punches with the heavy, steady flow of ice cold water cascading down onto us. Afterwards we were all invited to the local pub where chicken and chips in a basket were laid on, washed down with a couple of well-deserved pints.

I'll never forget those Saturday morning training sessions with Frank, Tony, Nigel, Kevin, Keith, Eddie, Martin and Bill and everyone else who used to train at that Dojo in the mid-seventies and eighties. Frank was a great teacher and an extremely good-natured man for whom I have the utmost respect. OSU!

Frank was building his empire and unfortunately that meant he had less and less time to give us lessons. The final straw for me came when a guy who had been only been at the club for a couple of years and was taking the lesson decided to omit the usual sparring session. Karate without our usual *kumite* (sparring)? What was the world coming to? This was becoming a regular occurrence – no

Frank, and no sparring. I made the sad decision to leave the karate school as I felt that no one else there could really teach me anything. I had been training there for about eight years and I had become very proficient. I had built up a strong mental and physical toughness that has served me well over the years.

I must admit I did miss the old place. I was going past there recently and had to pop in. I walked down the narrow gravel path and, to my surprise, the door was open. I went inside: the place was quiet and empty. I stood on the threshold of the doorway and thought about all those training sessions and all the people I'd met there. The dojo is still virtually exactly the same as it was the day I left all those years before.

CHAPTER TWO

Fighting Fit

After I left the karate club, I decided to build my own dojo/gym in my back garden, where my friends and I would be free to practice the way we wanted to and do as much sparring as we liked. I contacted a garage manufacturer who built the thing around my own design. Eventually I settled on it being fifteen feet long and ten feet wide. I had to make sure that it was built high enough for the punch bags, which were suspended from the thickest beam I could find – it was more or less a tree trunk. When it was all bolted together it looked absolutely superb.

Now that I had built the dojo, I needed to buy some equipment to put in it. We went to a place along the Fulham Palace Road called Mancini's, after the owner who was an old time boxing trainer. It's sadly no longer there now. It was a brilliant little shop and had everything you needed to equip a boxing gym. Andy, a mate of mine, drove Pete and myself down there to get the equipment. The only problem was that Andy had turned up in a green Citroen 2CV. It looked like a cross between a frog and a small green house on wheels.

The car was not exactly built for heavyweights either; we went around one corner on two wheels. I was sure the thing was going over at one point. It got us there and back though… just about. (I took the Tube the next time.)

A typical training session

We soon devised what we thought was a good routine. Here it is:

- A ten-minute warm up: stretching, callisthenics.
- One thousand jumps on the skipping rope.
- Three hundred press-ups in sets of fifty.
- Three hundred sit-ups.
- Left and right hooks non-stop on the heavy bag. For three rounds of three minutes.
- Combination punching on the heavy bag for one minute non-stop. Five times each.

After that we had some sparring matches, and then, to finish off, we practised our unarmed combat techniques.

We trained like that four times a week, every week. I felt that this was enough to get us into top condition: hard training without knocking our pipe out completely. We were now ready for anything.

We had a regular little crew who used to turn up. There was Little Tony, Pete, my old mate from my school big Peter, Andy and John. Tony was the smallest and lightest of the lads, but pound for pound the strongest. He trained like a demon and was as hard as a coffin nail. He could take a tremendous amount of punishment and still keep going forward.

Pete was six two and seventeen and a half stones and always trained hard. After a while he perfected an excellent left jab, one of the best I've seen (and felt).

Big Pete was the biggest and the heaviest of us at over eighteen stone and a touch over six two. He presented a formidable opponent. Initially he trained for many years in kung fu but adapted to boxing very well, I think I've still got a lump under my chin to prove it.

Andy was the new boy, weighing in at eleven stone and with no previous experience. He had to start from scratch, but was a fast learner and very game. He also never pulled a punch. He would try and knock your teeth out every time, which was good in a way because it kept you on your toes. In one match Andy received a really hard punch from Peter which resulted in a broken rib.

You know a little about my martial arts background, but boxing was something that came naturally to me. I studied a great deal of fight films; the fighters I used to watch most were Joe Louis and Rocky Marciano. Joe Louis was one of the best combination punchers ever and reigned for eleven years as the heavyweight champion of the world. Rocky Marciano has got to be the toughest boxer of all time: with his murderous right hand punch he defeated all comers and he was never beaten. He had forty-nine fights and recorded forty-nine wins with forty-three knockouts. He has remained the only world heavyweight champion in history to retire undefeated. These are the guys I would study to see how they delivered their punches and how they got themselves into position to unleash their devastating attacks.

I also studied a fighter called Jack Dempsey from the 1920s. His fight against the giant Jess Willard for the world heavyweight title was one of the most brutal ever to be shown on film. So with the Joe Louis combinations, Rocky Marciano's right hander, plus a bit of Jack Dempsey thrown in for good measure, I set about adopting their techniques and incorporating them into our training routines.

We trained hard, still using the training schedule. Press-ups, sit-ups, bag work and skipping were the fundamental building blocks. The sparring at the end of each session was as tough as I could make it. I felt it had to be made as real as possible. Quite a few schools that teach martial arts don't ever get anywhere near the kind of realism that you need for an actual encounter with someone. The person who has been training at a school that teaches a semi or a non-contact type of sparring is going to get battered big time in the real world. I call it the fantasy island syndrome.

Once a week we decided that one of us would stay up and fight for ten three-minute rounds. This was a great test of stamina, strength and spirit. One sparring match which springs to mind was with Pete. As usual it started off relatively normally and gathered momentum as it continued. Tony was doing the time-keeping. Pete was fighting really hard with absolutely no quarter. At the start of the third round, Pete caught me with a superb left jab, followed by another left into the rib cage, quickly followed by two more left jabs to the head. It put me on the defensive and I started to go backwards, but my training, determination and spirit kept me going: if you get caught in the solar plexus or floating ribs there's nothing you can do but cover up and weather the storm.

I was in the corner and under attack from Peter's persistent left jabs. I lured him in and waited for the right moment to counter-attack. I threw a fast left jab then a right cross combined with a hard left uppercut to the jaw, followed by a rib-crunching right hand to the body. It sent Pete crashing through the door of the gym and out into the back garden, where the fighting continued – much to the surprise of the builders who were putting in some double glazing next door. Two of them quickly turned around to see what was going on and almost fell off the scaffolding.

At that point Tony called a halt to the proceedings. Pete commented afterwards that when the upper cut landed on his chin, he thought he saw the sun and the moon rise simultaneously and that it was only sheer bloody mindedness and a refusal to give in that made him carry on. I call it spirit. You've got to be able to take it in the gym, because if you can't you will be in a lot of trouble in a real street fight.

The lads came in all shapes and sizes so you would be fighting someone who was six two, and the next time you would be fighting someone shorter and faster. That was good because in a real fight you can't pick and choose your opponent.

It was all done with the right kind of attitude and with absolutely no malice: in fact, quite the opposite. We had some right old punch ups in there. Believe it or not, it was all extremely enjoyable; we were all very fit and strong and could take the punishment. It was a great confidence builder as well. You see, I knew what the others didn't – I had drawn on what I had learned from the knock down fighting and tried to show the other guys that the sparring was intended to remove the fear of fighting. Basically we were not afraid of taking a few shots: if you can remove that fear and accept the fact that you may have to take a clump or two, violent confrontations are slightly easier to handle.

Sadly, Andy died in his late thirties. I've been thinking about him a lot during the writing of this book. He was a troubled character who found it difficult to handle the real world. We had some good laughs with Andy – he really was a likeable man. I did my best to help him when he was in trouble and I know that he appreciated my efforts. We drifted apart over the last few years and only bumped into one another very occasionally. I received my usual Christmas card from him and then found out four months later he was dead. John and I still make reference to him when we're training in the gym. If we hear an unexplained creak or a bang, or if the door will mysteriously open of its own accord, one of us will always say, "It's ok, it's only Andy mooching about."

Strange, isn't it? Only when someone is no longer around do you really begin to realise what you thought of them. Wish you were here, mate… But life goes on.

CHAPTER THREE

First Night Nerves

Friday 13th September 1993

My very first night on the door was for some guy who I worked with. He was arranging an eighteenth birthday party for his daughter and was concerned about things possibly being ruined by gate crashers. The venue was at a local cricket club. The party was to run from eight until twelve and was by invitation only, which would make life a bit easier. He paid up front; I think it was thirty quid. I needed a partner as it was a two man job, so my mate Pete volunteered to keep me company.

We were obviously as green as grass and didn't really know what we were doing or what to expect, this being our first night, but we'd worked out a few strategies in case it all went pear-shaped. Our philosophy was that we would treat people the way we would like to be treated ourselves, and anyone who gave us any attitude problems would get zero tolerance.

We put a great deal of thought and energy into finding the best ways in which we could eject troublemakers quickly and with as little fuss as possible. Not an easy thing to achieve. I studied a lot of restraining techniques from the karate and judo manuals that I'd accumulated over the years. My search through the numerous books led me to find a manual that I had completely forgotten about: it was called *All In Fighting*. It's a Second World War unarmed combat instruction booklet, with some very attention-grabbing techniques inside. Further research on this subject led us to discover a total immobilisation strangle and choke hold.

The trouble was that this jiu-jitsu technique was an extremely dangerous one and had to be used with caution. If you were to lock the hold on for too long or with too much pressure on the person's neck, it could cause serious injury – dislocation – or death. But the beauty of it was that if you performed it correctly, you got complete control over the transgressor. I practised it over and over. I consider myself to be very proficient in this particular method of restraint and over the years I've used it dozens of times (but only when necessary) without any problems.

The drawback to continuously practising these strangle holds was the wear and tear on the neck and throat area – we both had sore necks for a month. The only way to find out how effective your strangle holds and arm locks are is to execute them on your training partner, and vice versa. That way you get to know how much force is required to get the desired effect, namely compliance.

On the night of our first job, I picked Pete up at half seven. He jumped into the motor and we headed west into unknown territory. We arrived at the venue at about ten to eight. It was a beautiful late summer evening and as we pulled into the car park behind the cricket pavilion, a welcome cool breeze greeted us.

We made our way along the narrow straight path to the bar and once inside a short fat barman called us over.

"Are you two looking after the door for us tonight, then?" he said.

With that he produced two bottles of lager from the cold shelf. We thanked him for the beers and had a walk around the place. It was a rectangular-shaped sports hall. At one end people were busying themselves setting up a makeshift bar as the other one was off limits for the guests and at the other end the D J was plugging in his speakers and testing the microphone, "Testing, Testing, one, two, three, *screeeeeeeeeeeech*!"

Pete was savouring the last drops of his beer with a broad grin; he liked the occasional drink. We took up our positions either side of the door; black suit, white shirt, very smart. The family arrived and introduced themselves, and then the rest of the guests started to file past, each producing an invitation.

There must have been about a hundred or so in now. One woman, who was of rapidly advancing years, shall we say, kept looking over in Pete's direction. She approached him and whispered in his ear, "You're a big boy, are you big all over"?

"You can't half pick them mate," I said.

She was as rough as old Harry (whoever he was). I spoke too soon as she came over to me next. At the same time, this other old trout was dancing provocatively in front of Pete; she was gyrating her very large backside in his direction. Every now and then she would lift up the front of her dress, exposing her enormous thighs. She was stomping about like a young elephant. Once around her would be twice around the gas works.

Everyone was having a really good time as the party got into full swing. We had no trouble of any serious nature to deal with. The only problem we had was trying to hide ourselves from the attentions of the over-amorous old grannies. I don't think they had a full set of teeth between them.

"When are you two going to take us out for a drink, then?" one of them asked, winking at me with one of her mascara-encrusted eyes.

"They must have turned up on the wrong night. Grab-a-granny night is next week," I whispered to Pete.

"I bet your one's flattened a bit of grass in her time," Pete said, nodding to another over-the-hill admirer.

The only real irritating aspect of the night was the DJ. He kept coming over to us and saying that he'd done door work before and he was a kick boxer. He'd been in loads of fights, and not to worry because he'd steam in in good style if it kicked off… He wouldn't have been able to knock the skin off a rice pudding.

The evening passed with relative ease, and was actually quite a pleasant occasion. We made our escape through one of the rear fire exits to evade our two antiquated groupies, who were loitering with intent at the main entrance. We did a quick sprint across the car park and into the little Renault 5. I pointed the car in the direction of the A4 and home.

The next day we were at our regular place of work when the guy we'd done the security for the previous evening came over to thank us. He was very happy with the way the evening had gone and the way we'd conducted ourselves. He went on to say that after we'd left the venue, the DJ had been involved in a fight. He had received a right hander from a drunken old Pakistani bloke who had wandered into the cricket ground and found his way into the back of the DJ's van. And so the first of many nights on the door was a good one.

CHAPTER FOUR

THE SLOANE RANGERS

October 1993

A few weeks after our successful debut, we decided to have some business cards printed. Pete drafted a superb letter explaining our services. We would go for a bit of a mooch around the pubs and clubs in our local area and have a butchers at the door staff to see how they shaped up. If they were a bit scruffy or looked like a couple of wallies, we would put the place on our mailing list and send the manager our details. We received a few replies, but they were not offering the right money. Earning an extra few quid was the sole reason for our entering into this line of work; we weren't going to work for peanuts.

I want to explain at this point that we were not what you would call 'hard men', not sure what that actually means anyway. We didn't want to be, either. So I think that we entered into this with the right kind of attitude. But we were no mugs though.

The next job finally arrived, through a friend of a friend. We were asked to work the door at a private party in Chelsea. We agreed the money and hours, so the following Saturday evening we quickly changed into our black suits, switched on, and set off for West London. We decided to take the Tube, because parking in the area was a nightmare, plus with the traffic at that time in the evening it would have taken us ages to get there.

We were greeted by a steady pelting of heavy rain as we left the station and we quickly made our way through the long wet narrow high street, which eventually led us to the corner of the road. A right turn and three doors down and we arrived. Just as I was about to ring the bell, the door opened and inside the hallway was Philip. He was of medium height with grey thinning hair and a friendly smile.

"Hello boys, I've been expecting you. Now, I could pay now if you like or at the end. Which would you prefer?" Philip asked.

"I think now would be fine, thanks," I said as I held out my hand.

"How much did we agree?"

"It was forty-five quid each," I reminded him.

He pulled a wad of notes out from his pocket. He must have had at least a grand there.

"Well, here's fifty each. Come over here and have a drink," he said.

We followed him into the main room of the apartment. In the corner was a large plastic dustbin which was full of ice cubes and bottles of lager; he knocked the tops off two bottles and handed us one each. Over to our left was a large fireplace with a blazing log fire in it, so we stood in front of it for a while and dried ourselves off.

On the other side of the room was a huge dining table, about a third of it covered in champagne glasses. At the end of the table were two dozen bottles of the very best bubbly.

"What I want you to do is enjoy yourselves and imagine you are guests. The main reason I wanted you here is because a couple of the people I'm expecting can get a little boisterous after a few drinks, but I'm sure they'll behave once they know that I have you two boys around," Philip said.

He then asked us to go down to the basement, saying that he'd come and get us if anything happened. We went down a flight of stairs and into the basement, which was quite large, about twenty-foot square, and right in the middle was a pool table. We had a few games. After about half an hour, Philip came down to introduce us to one of his friends; his name was Johnny, the Earl of Something, a right eccentric character. He was tall and thin with dark shoulder-length hair. He was already pissed and obviously on something.

That was confirmed when he asked us if we wanted any "gear". He opened his jacket pocket and inside he had a substantial amount of pills and tablets in a variety of colours. Thanks, but no thanks; we were not interested, mate. I don't know what they were exactly, but I would imagine that after a couple of those you would be floating around the ceiling like a fucking mushroom. Mind-bending drugs were not our scene.

The majority of the people who showed up all spoke with that plum-in-the-mouth, ridiculous-sounding accent. The upper classes, old boy. Jolly good show and all that, what, what. You know the kind of people I'm talking about – they have that certain type of attitude with an outward show of imagined superiority. After a few drinks and a go of whatever else was on offer, their masks soon began to slip, exposing their true personalities. They then became like any other annoying drunk.

The two of us were fast becoming a bit of a curiosity. The guests were coming down to the basement just to have a look at the 'bouncers', especially the women, who were poking their heads around the doorway and giggling childishly while pointing in our direction.

A group of very attractive tipsy young women were all moving rhythmically to the latest dance music surrounded by Hooray Henrys, who were studying the form and guzzling champagne like it was going out of fashion. The women outnumbered the men buy at least two to one and the basement was definitely becoming the place to be. It was getting packed and a little rowdy when Johnny came running in to where we were, glass of champagne in one hand, spliff in the other, and said at the top of his voice, "You won't get any trouble, lads, just a few mad Sloane Rangers running around going 'Yar'! Yar! Yar!'"

A strange man, I thought.

It was getting far too crowded for us in the basement and the air was filling with the distinctive sickly smell of weed. So we decided to go upstairs where we could breathe a little easier. We stood at the back of the main room and positioned ourselves at either side of the large table, which was full of drinks and clean empty glasses. An attractive middle-aged woman flounced over toward Pete and engaged him in conversation. He thought she was coming over to chat him up, but what she actually said to him was that she would like two glasses of champagne and a bottle of lager. He'd decided to wear a bow tie for this particular function and she'd mistaken him for the waiter. I had to laugh as the bow tie came off in a flash.

There was lots of bedroom activity, and if the bedrooms were full they mooched about in the dark corners of the large conservatory.

At about midnight Philip came over to us and said that the two guys who were going to cause trouble had left as soon as they set eyes on us, and so that meant we were no longer on duty.

"Stay for the rest of the party as my guests, if you like, boys, or you can leave now if you prefer," a rather drunk Philip said.

Our job was done and so we decided not to hang around. If we were quick, we would be able to catch the last Tube train home.

Philip could not thank us enough. On our way out, I gave him one of our business cards. He took it and studied it under the lamp in the hall.

"Oh, that's fucking neat. Goodnight, lads."

As we were about to leave, one of the guests jumped out in front of us, barring our way to the front door.

"I want to take a picture of these two – they're the fucking stars of the party. Hic!"

Philip suggested he didn't take the photo and to step aside, as he wasn't sure how we were going to react.

"But I want to take a picture of them. Burp!"

Philip interjected again. "These lads duff people like you up for a living, so get out of the way." Philip said.

We boarded the train home, quite content with the evening's outcome. It had been a good night with no trouble at all, a couple of beers and a pizza, plus fifty quid each resting very happily in our pockets. We were hooked and hungry for more.

Throughout the journey home, a pissed Aussie had been casting the occasional glance over in our direction. He eventually said, "Are you two bouncers, then?"

He was referring to our black attire,

"No, we're with the Royal Philharmonic… so fuck off," I said.

CHAPTER FIVE
The PROFESSIONALS

December 1993

It had been a few weeks since our last engagement, so we changed the business cards to make them look a little more professional and then blitzed the pubs and clubs with them. This was all before the new strict licensing laws that are now in place, so in those days we were a bit of a law unto ourselves. Nowadays every door supervisor has to obtain a licence at some considerable cost and attend a course as well. This deals with first aid and firefighting, and explains such things as the licensing laws, powers of arrest and the use of reasonable force. I could go on, but it's getting boring.

We were not getting a very good response from our cards and letters idea so I decided to make a few follow-up phone calls. I rang the manager of the first pub we'd written to and asked for the name and number of the security company that they were using. Our idea was to find out if any of these pubs and clubs were unhappy with their security arrangements. If they were, we would then offer our services at a discount price. Virtually every place we contacted gave us the same company name. It looked like this little firm had most if not all of the contracts in the area. Well, if we couldn't beat them then we'd better join them. After Pete and I had a chat, we decided to give them a ring.

A fella with a Scots accent answered the phone.

"Hello, do you have any door supervisor vacancies at the moment?" I said.

"Aye well, before we start, I'll need to know if you've done this kind of work before?" he said with a slow, confident Glaswegian drawl.

"I've done a bit, and a mate of mine is also looking for some work".

"Right then, you'd better come down and see me for an interview".

We arranged to meet at three o'clock on the following Thursday. We brought two passport-sized photos each with us, as the guy had asked. They were the worst I'd ever seen Pete – looked like he'd just escaped from bloody Broadmoor in his.

The office was located in the basement of a large restaurant. There was a small spiral staircase leading down to the back door. I pressed the intercom and announced our arrival. I knew there was someone there on the other end, even though I didn't get a reply, and after a few seconds we heard the sound of the locks being released. Clank! Clank! Crunch! The last lock was opened.

A very large individual with a shaven square-shaped head opened the door. He opened it about six inches and presented his face in the gap. All that was missing was the bolt through his neck. He gave us a discerning look and then invited us in – not with words, he just beckoned us forward with his huge mitt. As we entered, we noticed a fella sitting behind a desk inside another smaller office over to our left. He looked up and stopped his phone conversation as we approached.

"Take a seat lads, I'll be with you shortly," he said.

I had a quick glance around the office. It was obviously a company in its infancy. It was quite a dingy place with no proper ceiling, just the exposed floor joists of the restaurant above. Nothing on the bare concrete floor either. At the other end of the office was a desk which was covered in papers. On the wall was a large notice board with the names of all the venues they were looking after cross-referenced with the people who were looking after them. The guy behind the desk introduced himself to us with a firm handshake.

"Hello boys, how are you doing? My name is John," he said, and then asked us if we had our photos. "Aye now, that's a very good likeness." He grinned whilst holding up Pete's photo.

We stayed and chatted for a while, and after about twenty minutes he said that he would be in contact with us in a few days. He seemed decent enough. I'm a pretty good judge of character usually, and he seemed like a very genuine sort of bloke. He gave the impression that you wouldn't want to get on the wrong side of him, though. I also got the feeling that there was definitely more to these people than met the eye. The not-very-well-hidden pump action shotgun in the corner might have been the clue. We'll see how it goes.

As we were leaving, I noticed that a door off to our right was slightly ajar. It was a large room that they had turned into a gym, complete with punch bags and various other pieces of training equipment. They even had a bloody boxing ring set up down there. We couldn't resist the temptation; Pete held the punch bag and I threw a few boxing combinations at it.

John phoned back a week later and asked if Peter and I would like to work Saturday night.

"Ok mate, where do want us to go?" I asked.

He gave me the location and I asked my usual question.

"What's the money like?"

"How does £90 a piece sound?"

"Sounds fine mate, we'll be there."

"You will have to be there from 10pm till about 8am".

Kings Cross was our destination. We boarded the early evening train and left the leafy suburbs of Ealing behind. Forty-five minutes later we arrived. Dreary and depressing summed the place up, a run-down inner city dump where every vice imaginable was on offer.

As we exited the station, the police were everywhere. Six of them were trying to arrest some black guy who was brandishing a large carving knife and taunting them with it. It took them ages to deal with the situation; we were tempted to go over and show them how it should be done. Mind you, they would have probably nicked us for being too rough with the gentleman. Eventually they all jumped on him and then he was very gently placed in the back of the police van. I thought that they were far too hesitant with the guy. Anyone who carried a weapon of that nature and then decided to use it should get absolutely no mercy.

I don't know what training the police received, but it all looked very amateurish and haphazard from where we were standing. A lot of luck was involved.

We were half an hour too early and so we set off in search of the nearest battle cruiser. We found a pub close to the venue. It had a few Hell's Angels mooching about inside but they didn't take much notice of us. The music was excellent. As we walked in the jukebox was playing one of my favourite pieces of heavy rock music, 'Paranoid' by Black Sabbath.

Two halves of lager later and it was time to shoot over the road.

The venue was, and still is, a very popular place: three massive warehouses linked together with enough room for thousands of revellers. As we entered, John was standing in the main entrance.

"You made it then, lads?" he said, checking his watch.

"Hello mate, what's happening?" I replied.

"You two come with me."

We followed him down a flight of stairs and along a corridor to where we were to spend the majority of the night. We were then introduced to the other member of the company who jointly ran it with John.

"All right lads," said John. "If you'd like to listen in."

He then proceeded to show us how to search someone for any drugs or weapons. Everyone was to be searched without exception. We were to ask them if they had any needles on them, then search their hats, boots, bags – everything. John explained that underneath the collar on a shirt or jacket was one of the favourite hiding places for small amounts of drugs. He demonstrated the search technique on one of the staff.

"Start at the top and work down. Tell them to raise their arms, feel down each of the sleeves.

Ask them to remove any head gear; if they refuse, turf them out of the line. Then do the collar, and over the shoulders and around the back. Next grab hold of the waistband of the trousers and give them a good shake – you never know, something might fall out – then down the inside of legs, then the outside and finally the footwear. Ask them to take them off if you feel it's necessary."

If we found any drugs – sorry, *when* we found any drugs – we were to put them into a steel drugs box which was taken to the local police station the next day. (Most of the contents, anyway.)

A few minutes later the first of the night's revellers started to arrive. We were stopping and searching the punters for a good couple of hours. I must have done about three hundred squats as I searched people down to their boots: we had most definitely drawn the short straw.

Two huge queues formed which stretched right back to the high street: guys on the left and the girls on the right. There were hundreds of scantily-clad, noisy young females, scruffy-looking dudes and undesirables of every description descending on the place. A couple of old Trannies were parading themselves up and down the never-ending ranks of impatient young people. They were dressed in over-elaborate costumes, trying to amuse the punters who were having to wait forever to gain entry. The inescapable thump, thump, thump of the dance tracks blasted out as we frisk the crowd.

The guy who had organised the event, and who, incidentally, was dressed in a long flowing purple gown topped off with a witch's hat, was making himself very busy. He was flitting about in an exited fashion with an over-the-top foppish manner, giving orders left, right and centre with animated gestures like some kind of demented orchestral conductor.

Pete suddenly turned towards me as he was searching the lower half of some shabby fella. His face had the expression of someone who had just taken a bite out of very bitter lemon.

"What's up, mate?" I asked.

"I'll tell you later," he said.

And so about ten minutes later, we eventually got a break.

"What happened when you were searching that bloke?" I asked Pete.

Pete explained that while he was searching around the back of the guy's trousers, he'd discovered that the fella had shit his pants. Two things sprang to my mind. The first was that this fella was now going to be wandering around all night with his pants full of shite. Secondly, Pete had had his hand around the back of this bloke's trousers and he was now munching away on a cheese and pickle sandwich, using the same unwashed hand.

After our well-deserved break, we were asked to patrol for the rest of the night, which was a welcome relief from the search area. As we strolled through the crowds, the sickly bittersweet smell of puff was inescapable. This place was rough and, except for the strobe lights, it was really dark in there.

Whilst doing our patrol we observed some curious sights. Some individuals were very lively and jigging about furiously on the same spot, head down, looking at the floor. Some of them were just standing and staring wide-eyed into space, open-mouthed with blank expressions and soaked in sweat and out of their heads. If that was their idea of a good night out, they could keep it.

It was absolutely boiling; someone must have turned the heating on full blast. The best little earner must have been the water concession. Whoever had that must have made a fortune with a small bottle of water at £1 a pop.

The revelry thankfully began to draw to a close at around four o'clock. We were cream-crackered and wanted out. By six o'clock the end was in sight. A twenty-five strong team of bouncers formed ranks and drove the remnants of the crowd into one area and gradually steered them towards the main exit. The snatch squads had had a busy night intercepting drugs and the dealers. Above the dance floor, if you could call it that, was an elaborate system of walkways where spotters would be hiding. They would carry a radio and a laser pointer with them, and when a deal was in progress they would radio through the details to the snatch team whilst keeping the red laser dot on the dealer's nut. When they were caught, the dealers and their customers were given very rough treatment and were literally kicked out.

We waited in line outside the office while John sorted out the cash and eventually we were called in. John paid us a bit extra and we collected a hundred and twenty quid each and then wearily set off towards the station and home. That was good money back then. You'd be hard pressed to better it nowadays.

I think we did that venue three or four times. The money was good but I never liked the place. However, John the guv'nor had now seen how we operated and wanted us there more often. After our stint at the little club in West London, he would often get on the dog and bone and ask us to come up to Kings Cross. Some of the guys loved it there but it wasn't for me. I had *bad vibes* every time I set foot in the place. I had a feeling that something was going to go badly wrong here one night. Unfortunately my prediction proved to be right: one night, about six months after our debut there, a member of the snatch team was stabbed to death on the premises whilst trying to apprehend a drug dealer. A young man's life was brutally and savagely taken away for the sake of a few lousy quid.

Many doormen have been killed in the line of duty. It's a statistic that I feel will only sadly increase, especially with today's growing gun and knife culture and the willingness of these thugs to commit murder with very little if any provocation. When they are caught, they are awarded a sentence that rarely befits the crime and they will probably only serve two thirds of it anyway.

We need stronger laws in place for people who carry knives. There was a report in the newspaper recently about a young boy who was out on an errand at the local shop for his mother and was stabbed to death for his mobile phone. Words fail me: I cannot express how I feel about such things. Imagine the devastation on the family – it's just too terrible to comprehend

If I had my way, I would reintroduce the death penalty for such crimes. The person who takes a life in a premeditated, cold-blooded attack with a knife has to pay the ultimate price. Anything less than that and I feel that justice has not been served. There's no margin for error with a knife: they are simply designed to kill. Unfortunately, the reality is that these cold, sick people do exist and they are out there with knives at the ready. So after that tragic incident, I decided that we had to be ready to defend ourselves against the knifer.

CHAPTER SIX
STREET FIGHTING MAN

January 1994

To combat our concerns over possible knife attacks, we firstly acquired bullet/stab-proof vests. I spoke to John about it and the very next week he had a stack of stab-proof vests sitting in the corner of his office, which he sold to the team at a hugely discounted price. I still have the thing in my wardrobe.

In addition to the vest, I set about reading every knife self-defence manual I could lay my hands on. We studied the techniques that seemed to be the most effective and adopted the most uncomplicated methods and incorporated them into our training routine. We practised them over and over until they became second nature. I remember we started off by using a real knife when practicing: it was a bloody great flick knife, a scary-looking thing, with a thin, shiny six-inch blade. This was the real deal and when confronted with a real knife, even in practice with your mate on the other end of it, it puts a completely different aspect on things. Your senses are automatically heightened and, dare I say, 'sharpened' when that silver flashing blade with death written all over it comes thrusting at you.

Even though I trusted my training partners implicitly, accidents happen and I was almost skewered by the damned thing one day. I only just managed to parry the blade away from an intimate date with my liver at the last moment. After that we decided to use a rubber knife.

One of the most important things I learnt about knife self-defence was the seizing of your attacker's knife hand, and not letting go of it. You literally hang on for dear life. Parrying seemed to work also. Keeping it simple is the name of the game. And running away is always a good idea… if you think you can.

I have given a lot of thought to putting together a practical self-defence manual. Not like some that you see with the use of flamboyant kicks and complicated blocking routines – they would probably get you killed if you tried to use them against someone who had a knife. My manual deals with the reality of what is required to subdue your attacker so you can make your escape and survive the ordeal. (The book is called *The Modern Warrior*.)

I have worn a covert Kevlar vest ever since the incident at Kings Cross. Such vests are not cheap but they are an obviously essential piece of kit. I advise anyone involved in any type of security occupation to obtain one. Another piece of kit we used to wear was a groin guard, again for obvious reasons, and I always had a pair of good quality leather gloves. Mine were knife-proof: they were ordinary leather gloves but with Kevlar inserts. We wore boots as opposed to shoes, the reason being is that they don't accidentally come off. Pete was going in to deal with a fight one night, closely followed by me. I inadvertently trod on the back of his shoe and it came flying off. He was hopping around in the dark for a good few minutes trying to find it. By the time he had retrieved it, the situation had been dealt with.

So now we were as ready as we could be to deal with any situation that came our way. However, confrontations can happen when you least expect them, and are not always confined to the entrance of the nightclub.

It was a normal Monday afternoon... I had finished a particularly tough two-hour training session, and so I went through the usual routine: a hot bath followed by something to eat, and then I planned to get my head down for a couple of hours. But this time my sleep was interrupted by some really loud knocking on my front door. I went downstairs and opened the front door to find a guy wanting to deliver some new kitchen equipment.

As I looked out and up the garden path, his mate was coming down with it on a trolley. I have four steps leading down to my front door and he banged it down every one of them. As he got to the front door, I said to him that if it didn't work, I'd know why.

"Don't worry about it, man, it's tightly packed," was his reply.

They eventually brought the stuff through and I asked them if they could unpack it and also take the packaging with them. The driver had no problems with my request, but the other guy, a tall lean black fella, was moaning about it.

"We're not supposed to do this," he moaned and started to walk out with a right strop on. As he walked past me, he looked at me with a stupid half sneer.

"Have you got a problem, mate?" I said.

"No, you got the problem, man."

As he turned around, he looked at me and told me to fuck off. How rude.

SMACK!! A hard, fast right hand punch knocked him off the doorstep onto his back and he landed amongst the flowers in the front garden some five or six feet away. I have never seen anyone more surprised; the look of absolute disbelief on his face was amazing. I think he was the type of guy who rarely had anyone stand up to him, let alone smack him straight in the eye. I'll not have anyone talk to me like that, especially on my own doorstep. I'm not a great talker in these types of situations. Anyway, I'd made up my mind, as I knew that talking to this fella would have gotten me nowhere. Either take the shit that he's chucking and do nothing, or do something about it. So the dialogue went out the window and he went out of the door and landed on his back!

As I stepped outside to finish him off, he was getting to his feet. He was in a crouched position, leaning forward with his arms waving about in front of him. His legs were doing a funny little dance. Clearly his noodle had been quite badly shaken by the punch and so I closed in on him. I threw a left hook and right upper cut combination; they both missed the target.

He must have felt the wind of the upper cut as it went past – it was literally millimetres away from hitting him. However, I'd put so much power into the upper cut, I lost my balance and I fell backwards over the dustbin and landed flat on my back. So at this stage I was doing a pretty good job of beating myself up. My opponent had by now regained some, or most, of his senses and he saw his opportunity for some payback. He dived on top of me and whacked me in the face with a big bunch of keys, two of which were protruding from between his fingers. The blow opened a cut over my right eye.

No matter how hard I tried, I couldn't get to my feet because the dustbin was wedged under the backs of my legs. And then bang! He caught me again in the same spot, but his blows lacked any real power. I think that the clump I'd given him had taken away his strength. I brought my knee up and managed to wedge my foot into his stomach and push him off. I then tried again to get to my feet but that fucking dustbin was still well and truly on his side.

He came for me once again, trying to finish me off this time. He rushed in and leant over me, his fist raised. The blood from the gash under his eye was dripping all over my white t-shirt. He thought he was in control and took a swing at me with his keyed fist, but I managed to catch him with a blow under the eye which opened the gash a little more. It unzipped like a purse and disgorged a fair amount of blood. He jumped back and that gave me the chance to finally get to my feet. I rolled to the side, and as

I got into my fighting stance, he did a runner and hurdled the front gate.

I was willing to leave it at that, but he decided to pick up a brick and throw it in my direction. It missed me but hit the window frame, which cracked the glass. For the first time during the whole encounter, I completely lost my temper. My front door was open, and just inside the hallway, on the floor, I saw the claw hammer I'd been using to hang some pictures up the day before. I grabbed the hammer to go after him but my wife gripped my arm to stop me. I looked at her and then looked back toward the front gate and he was flying along the road in the van.

There was some police involvement, but we managed to agree to disagree as to what had actually happened, and when the police arrived I told them nothing. They phoned me a little later that day and I asked what the score was. The detective on the other end of the phone said that the chap had received ten stitches in his eye and wanted to see if I was going to pursue the matter.

"So are you going to press any charges, sir? If so, the gentleman said he will as well; he's sitting here with me now."

"No, no charges, but tell him he fights like a girl, will you?" I said

He put the phone down and that was that.

I learned two important lessons from that incident:
1. Always put your boots on: I had a really bad cut on the underside of my right foot.
2. Move the dustbins out of the way.

CHAPTER SEVEN
CHAV TOWN

February 1994

I received a phone call from John asking if I wanted to work the door that weekend. The venue was a rough pub in a town called Sunbury. There would be two of us to look after the governor down there as he was being intimidated. The brief was that there was a little firm in the pub that was taking liberties, hassling customers, dealing and refusing to pay for drinks etc.

Pete was having the weekend off, and so for the first time my back was going to be watched by a total stranger. One the most important things in this game is being able to trust the person you're working with. Working with people you don't know can be very costly. You have no idea how they are going to react when situations get ugly. Their bottle could go when you need them to watch your back, and then you'll be left standing there like lemon on your Jack.

I arrived at the venue with more than a little trepidation. I opened the door to the pub and I was immediately approached by a tall lean fella with a Kiwi accent.

"Hello mate, I'm Chris," he said as he offered his hand.

My initial level of apprehension was now almost completely gone and I was somewhat relived by his presence, and he mine I think. Sometimes you meet someone and you almost immediately know whether or not they are kosher. I knew that this guy was not the type who would back down; his casual friendly manner with the punters was all a front, and a good one.

The pub was big and was situated right in the middle of a large council estate. It was a traditional old fashioned looking place, complete with a smelly, threadbare, beer-stained patterned carpet and a light brown nicotine-coated ceiling.

The DJ was in the corner setting up his 'disco' equipment, which consisted of a turntable that sat upon what looked like a modified ironing board flanked on either side by some DIY flashing light units. I was then introduced to the landlord, who was a short-arse mouthy little prick and absolutely fitted right in with the place. I didn't know who was worse – him or the punters.

You would have been hard pressed to find a place with a more concentrated amount of scumbag chavs: it was wall to wall with attitude. You have to use your loaf a bit in places like this, because if you give one of these punters a slap, you'll probably end up fighting everyone in the pub. Basically the people that frequented the place just wanted to cause us as much grief as possible. They really thought they owned the place and we were the enemy.

As the place started to fill I was getting some curious looks which made me feel about as welcome as pork chop at a Jewish wedding. Thankfully we had nothing too serious to deal with. Except that, toward the end of the night, I began to receive the usual mindless comments from the morons and the fantasy island armchair warriors. I'd heard all of this well-rehearsed alcohol-fuelled rhetoric before.

"What are you fucking bouncers doing in 'ere?" a short-arsed grubby crackhead said as he stood directly in front of me in a gunfighter-type pose.

"You fink you're so fucking 'ard," was the passing comment from a chubby, young blonde woman as she waddled past me on high heels.

"I reckon I could 'ave you, mate. A few years ago I'd have done you up a treat, old son," claimed the old pisshead as he stumbled out of the door.

"You're a big bloke, but that don't bother me because I know people," the old pisshead's mate said while pointing at me.

And then my all-time favourite:

"I'll come back and do you, mate, and I've got guns as well," a forty-something-year-old drunk said for no apparent reason as he swayed about in front of me.

Fucking losers, I thought.

CHAPTER EIGHT

MY MANOR

John's secretary rang me and asked if Pete and I would come down to the office for a chat.

Why wasn't John calling? I thought. I knew that they were a dodgy little firm and I was never a hundred percent sure about them. Why would they want to see us at the office? It could be that we'd somehow fallen foul of them. Or it could be that we were about to be further indoctrinated into their organisation.

I had heard that a couple of weeks back one of their brethren had been caught with his hand in the till and he'd been given a terrible beating. So we decided to tool up in case it all went Pete Tong.

I'm pleased to say that the meeting was a good one and was concerning an offer of a more permanent position within the company, which we were delighted to accept. Along with our wages, we had gone up in their estimation and we were now considered part of the firm.

The venue that we were going to look after was in a very affluent part of West London where you could occasionally rub shoulders with the rich and famous. Ironically it was one of the places that we had contacted with a view to employment a while back. It was a beautiful area during the day with its large picturesque green where, centuries ago, tournaments and pageants were held. It had clusters of wonderful little antique shops and cosy pubs and restaurants that meandered along the broad curve of the wide high street. The end of the high street led you down towards the river. It was a tranquil, classy little town. However, after six o'clock, and once the shops had battened down the hatches for the night, the place took on a different kind of atmosphere. Hordes of youngsters and all kinds of weirdos crawled out of the woodwork and descended upon it.

It was quite a pleasant-looking bar. It was a big red-brick building, which back in the day was once an elegant hotel. I looked up at the elaborate stone sign above which said: 'The Railway Hotel 1888'. The long façade of the bar was lit by a dozen sturdy brass lamps. The lamps were suspended above the large arched windows that overlooked the high street. Each powerful lamp deposited a shaft of bright white light onto the heads of the patrons queuing outside. A curved emerald green sunshade hung above the front doors. We were both unusually quiet and a little tense for some reason. I'm not sure why, but the feeling was almost palpable; maybe deep down we both secretly didn't what to be there?

We'd arrived a little too early and had gone for a coffee in the fast food restaurant next door to kill some time. After about fifteen minutes we decided to show our faces. We turned the corner, and standing at the door, bathed in a defused pool of yellow light, was a young fair-haired pretty little Scotswoman. She greeted us with a warm smile, introduced herself and gave us a friendly handshake. Her name was Joyce and she'd been the manager here for the past three years. She had no idea that a couple of months beforehand I'd been speaking to her on the phone about our possible takeover bid for the door here. I kept shtum.

***

I liked the fact that there were four of us on that door, although that dwindled to two after a while. The two other boys, Dave and Mark, were both very experienced doormen. They were confident and gave the impression that they could definitely handle themselves. The club had an alarm system with strategically placed alarm buttons; one was just inside the front doors on the floor, so a discreet tap with your toe would summon the rest of the boys when things were going pear-shaped. The set up was two in-house and two front of house, and then we'd switch around after half an hour or so.

There was also one up by the DJ who, incidentally, was a right prima donna. And definitely was more trouble than he was worth. The other thing that annoyed me about him was that he was on a good deal more than money us. Surely it should have been the other way around. Mind you, we used to give him a bit of stick, especially if he started to play that RnB music. One of the lads had a quiet word with him one night and he seemed to be as good as gold after that. I never found out what was actually said to him, but he was always very well behaved when this particular doorman was around. If I were to hazard a guess as to what was said, it probably had something to do with him, his equipment and a large plate glass window.

The type of music that a venue played was important: it set the tone of the club, thereby attracting a certain type of punter and, more importantly, discouraging another. There was some really good dance and house music around at the time. Robin S, The Nightcrawlers and 'Dreamer' by Livinjoy and 'The Bomb' by the Bucketheads were my own personal favourites at the time. They all still sound just as good today.

The other security position was by the toilets – not the most sought-after position, but an important one as most of the drug deals would go down in there.

As I entered the club for the first time, the deep thudding dance track started. The lighting began flashing and spinning in sync with the beat of the dance track, and the dry ice machine was puffing out a thin white mist. Over to my left there was a large L-shaped bar with eight TV screens above it, which played endless music videos all night long. Dead ahead was a small dance floor, and beyond that a little staircase that led you up to a raised platform which was where the DJ was positioned.

There was also a large conservatory area with a pool table, and a sizeable beer garden. At the time it was the most popular club in the area. Little did I know when I turned up that first night that I would be on that door for the next four years. I'd also become the head doorman in a short space of time. I would experience some happy and sad occasions, engage in lots of small fights and some that were pretty rough. I had my courage put through the mangle and wrung out to dry many times, but I'm pleased to say that I never did back down from the bullies, drunks and self-styled hard men. I had a few laughs along the way as well though.

A night club is a place where anything can happen – good and bad. These are places where you can lose your mind, body, soul and teeth in one fell swoop. The sights, the sounds, the smells and the neon lights draw the exited young punters like moths to a flame.

The first things you see are the tough-looking bouncers at the front door, confident and expressionless with their arms folded, all standing in their hint-of-danger poses. The queue begins to form as the moths start to gather. A group of seductive pretty girls with everything on show are at the head of the queue, the loud and boisterous group of young fellas behind them, a dodgy dealer is stalking them close by. A couple of the local hard men swagger past, their slits for eyes searching the queue for easy prey. They are all symbiotic: all one and part of it all.

The DJ sets the thumping soundtrack in motion which dictates the feel-good vibe; the irresistible atmosphere has now been now created. Inhibitions will be lowered, skirts will be hoisted, knickers will be dropped and defences will be breached as the alcohol and drugs kick in. It's futile to resist, you will be sucked in. The powerful narcotic will work its magic on you and you will succumb. We are watching. It's the world in microcosm.

***

Three months on

We'd had nothing too serious to contend with, just a lot of verbal. Mark had moved on – he'd decided to get involved in some close protection work. Dave had left too, which was a shame because we got on really well with him. He was a pleasure to work with and was 100% reliable and trustworthy.

We got a succession of different guys turning up as replacements. The first one was Garry, a stocky bald-headed cockney fella – a nice guy but far too aggressive with the punters. He lacked the diplomacy you need to have in this line of work. He was a kind of floater and would be used to plug the gaps when others failed to turn up for work or were on holiday.

The next week we had Alex with us. He was a big, tall Scots lad. His hair was black as a raven, he was square-jawed and was a tough-looking guy. And with that Glaswegian drawl he came across as a real hard man, which he was, but sometimes he could be as nice as hell. But once again, he was far too aggressive when it wasn't really necessary. I think he and Garry just didn't give a toss, but the problem was that their actions could also drag you down with them. I think they thought that because they were with Peter and I (two big lumps), they could get away with taking a few liberties.

One lovely warm summer Saturday evening, Pete, Alex and your humble narrator were all on the front doors in shirt-sleeve order. The queue was starting to form and the place was beginning to get busy. A young, white-faced nervous barman suddenly appeared and asked if we could have a word with some fella inside who was getting a bit abusive. He pointed him out and Pete asked him to behave. The right response was not forthcoming and so he was asked to leave.

"Fuck off, I ain't going anywhere," he said.

Now we had little choice as he'd refused to leave willingly but there were ways, techniques if you like, of how to get trouble makers out of the place with as little disruption as possible. I remained where I was at the front doors. Pete grabbed the fella by one arm and Alex grabbed him by the other and the drunk was thrown out of the door. I was dealing with the crowd queuing up but I caught a sight of the guy flying past me from a really hard shove off the step from Alex.

The guy looked like a right nutter. He was in a wrinkled old tartan shirt, scruffy jeans and dirty training shoes. I was looking for his banjo; he looked like an extra from the film *Deliverance*.

He stood there glaring at me from about five or six feet away. His teeth were clenched, his chin was jutting out at a peculiar angle and his neck was stretched to its limit. His bloodshot eyes were bulging out and staring right at me.

I didn't mind – eyes cannot hurt you and he was outside my exclusion zone. I used to visualize a chalk circle of about four feet in circumference on the ground around me: anyone entering that was too close and was in perfect kicking range. He hadn't entered it yet and so didn't present a problem at the moment. He stood there staring for what seemed like an age so eventually I spoke up.

"Hey, mate, we don't want any trouble, now do we, so why don't you go home?"

There was no reply from him and no movement. I left him to it, thinking he'd get fed up with this after a while and disappear of his own accord. Just then, Alex arrived at the front doors and stuck his head out of the doorway.

"Are you still here?" If you don't fuck off, I'll batter you all around the fucking street," Alex said, while pointing at the fella.

"Fuck off, you Scots git," the bloke replied.

Here we go, I thought, as I backed off and leant up against the wall, facing our friend.

As the guy made a sudden dash for the door, Alex's hairy forearm flashed past my nose; his fist was on a direct collision course with the guy's skull. It sounded like a cricket ball hitting a coconut when it struck. The guy went down flat on his back and landed about six feet away from me, but almost immediately jumped up again and looked straight at me. He was now really pissed off. His face reddened as he let out a scream like in those war films when the army are doing their bayonet training.

"AAAARRRRGH!" he screamed and he charged forward.

He came rushing at me, but I remained perfectly still. I was relaxed with my eyes trained on him, range-finding. I waited for him to cross the imaginary chalk line, and when he entered the 'zone', I released the mother of all front kicks with a loud "Kiai!" He ran straight into the powerful kick. My size eleven right boot connected perfectly and momentarily disappeared into the soft centre of his belly: the force of the kick literally bent him in two.

His feet left the ground and he was now airborne and heading backward in the direction he had come from. Landing about five feet away on his back for the second time that night, he was winded, dazed and confused. He stayed down and was doubled up in pain when we got to him. We quickly flipped him over and put him into two very painful arm locks. Unluckily for him, a copper happened to be passing by at that moment and asked our mate on the floor, "What are you going to do if these nice gentlemen let you go?"

"I'm going to fight them," he said as he began to recover.

He was then given a nice pair of shiny government-issue bracelets to wear and was thrown into the back of a waiting police van. The copper came back about an hour later and told us that he felt sorry for him and had let him go because, as they approached the nick, he started to cry and promised to go home.

We noted a few problem areas at the club that needed addressing. The place wasn't that bad trouble-wise, but there was room for improvement. There just needed to be a little tweaking here and there.

The club had one or two local hard men who'd made it their own. We'd clocked them, made a mental note of them and decided that they simply had to go. They were cocky and arrogant and quite a violent little bunch who attracted the wrong kind of people. Pete and I were now on a mission – a mission to clean up this here town! (Spits into imaginary spittoon.)

We were determined that things were going to change for the better as we had planned on sticking around for a while. This was our club now: we were in control. We had a quick briefing and then took the place by the scruff of its fucking neck. But it wasn't going to be easy: these creatures weren't going to give up without a fight. 'No hats, no jeans, no trainers' the new sign on the wall said. Our plan was to sweep the rubbish away and literally clean the house and therefore create a new, vibrant, safe night spot for the decent people out there. So that night we put operation 'Zero Tolerance' into effect.

First on the list was a loudmouth, very aggressive Asian bodybuilder. He was a strong-looking fucker and was as wide as he was tall. He was a bit of a nutter as well and was always fighting and causing problems. With his square head and mop of thick black hair and tough features he was instantly recognisable at the back of the queue. As he got closer, it looked as if someone had played a game of noughts and crosses on his forehead with a knife.

Your card is marked, my old son, I thought as he passed by.

It didn't take long, and about an hour later three skinheads decided to throw their weight around. They began to have a go at the Asian fella and his wife. Now, this fella could look after himself but his wife tore into them with language that would have put Bernard Manning to shame.

We were watching the proceedings unfold and we could see that the Asian fella was now fronting the three skinheads up. He started shouting and screaming at them and they were doing the same back to him. Meanwhile his wife was continuing to give them a good volley of verbal as well. *Time to put an end to it,* I thought.

I quickly moved in and stood between the warring parties. I managed to calm the Asian guy down and escort him and his wife out of the front doors. To tell you the honest truth, I wanted him to have a pop at me because he was the sort of bloke who really deserved a pasting, but I couldn't justify it as it was the three lads behind me who were the aggressors and not him, on this occasion. *His time will come,* I told myself as I turned my attention to the three skins behind me.

The skinheads continued to cause more trouble and begin going after the guy, shouting some more abuse. *What's wrong with these people?* The couple were outside now and walking away. Pete and I turned around to deal with three skinheads, who were all laughing at the thought that they had got the Asian fella thrown out of the club. I went to who seemed to be the ringleader and asked him to put his drink down and leave.

"What for? Fuck off, mate," he said, and waved his hand dismissively in my direction.

As soon as his last words left his lips, my right hand was on his throat and my left hand slapped down on his right wrist. His hand was still holding onto a pint glass. There was no point in trying to appeal to their good nature: they had deliberately come here to cause trouble and no amount of good-intentioned talking was going to make any difference.

Once you have made the decision to eject someone, you have got to be totally committed. A half-hearted effort will only give your adversary the opportunity to counter-attack and then *you* will be on the receiving end.

If you go in 50% committed you will probably end up by getting 100% battered.

I started to push the guy backwards towards the front doors. A silence had now descended over the crowd and they parted like the Red Sea for Moses. Halfway he started to wriggle out the grip I had on his throat. He dug his heels in and we came to a halt. A *Muay* Thai knee strike to his ribcage doubled him over and I was able to get him going backwards again. I manoeuvred him over to the doors, and as I was doing so, his mate tried to attack me with a beer glass. Pete grappled with him and then the third guy came at me from the other side.

I switched my grip from the guy's throat into a headlock, and at the same time I swung my other arm around his mate's neck. So I had the pair of them in headlocks now. I managed to wrestle them both into the doorway. Pete shoved the other guy outside, and in the melee the ringleader was thrown to the ground. He sat on the floor like a spoilt little kid and went into a tantrum. He started to rant and rave about how he was going to come back and sort us all out. What he actually said was, "I'm going to come back and stick a big fucking knife through your head." He was pointing at me whilst he said it.

I grabbed hold of him by the collar of his jacket and dragged him unceremoniously out of the doorway and into the street.

"You're all barred, now fuck off," I said, and that was that.

Joyce has a discreet word with me later on.

"Well done for dealing with those guys. If at any time you want to take someone down into the cellar to give them a good hiding, feel free to do so."

To look at her you would think butter wouldn't melt in her mouth… I liked Joyce.

The Asian fella and his wife turned up at around closing time looking for the skinheads. They were both really drunk and very loud. They started to have a heated argument outside the entrance to the club. The fella grabbed his wife by the lapel and raised his fist. It didn't look as if this was the first time that they'd had this type of altercation. She then smashed a beer bottle on the railings and threatened him with it, promising that if he didn't back off he would be sorry. Joyce was watching what was happening and said that she wanted these two barred.

"Yeah ok, Joyce, will do," I said.

Little did she know that we were already going to do it.

Two weeks later...

Pete offered to go and get the teas from the fast food restaurant next door and left his position up on the little stage area next to the DJ. This was, incidentally, the best place to scrutinize all the crumpet from, and Pete could be frequently found there. I was now alone on the front door. Just as Pete disappeared, the Asian guy turned up with three of his pals and he approached the entrance.

"Sorry mate, you're barred. You'll have to drink somewhere else," I said and held out the palm of my hand halting them.

"Leave it out, we've been coming here for years. Why am I fucking barred, then?"

He stepped a little closer and I could see that he became a little wary. I'm not a body builder, but I was a good deal taller than him and similar in width. I tried to be as diplomatic as possible and explained that it was because of the argument he'd had with his wife a couple of weeks ago.

"I'm going in to see if my wife's in there," he said.

"You're not going in, and she's not in there anyway," I said.

"How do you fucking know that?" He was becoming more aggressive. I could see that his adrenaline was kicking in as his speech became a little less coherent. I remained calm: if the truth be told, I reckoned I could have taken him apart, but I didn't really want too. By now my patience was beginning to wear a little thin.

"She's not in there because she's barred as well," I said.

With that he started to lose his temper and shaped up as if he wanted to have a go. He swaggered forward. His friends took hold of him by the arms in an effort to restrain him. I had seen him involved in a brawl a while back when I'd been passing by in the car, and he gave a pretty good account of himself. He had some fella up against the wall and was punching the guy with short fast uppercuts to the face. Having had enough of his insults and threats, I asked his companions to release him.

"If he wants to have a go, we'll have a straightener," I said.

I knew exactly which technique I was going to use. He was probably only about five nine. I was standing on the step, and so the moment he stepped into the old exclusion zone, it'd be lights out for him. As soon as he was in range, he was going to get a size eleven toe punt right under the chin. Luckily for him, his friends pulled him away. At that moment, Pete the tea boy arrived.

CHAPTER NINE
THE KNIFE MAN COMETH

I got on well with the local constabulary… on the whole. We were at the front doors one evening, in our usual places, when a guy came out from the bar and informed us that some fella, whilst in the middle of a game of pool, had placed a large knife on the side of the table. I think there was a few quid on the game and so he was trying to intimidate his opponent. We went in, and as one of the other lads talked to the guy to distract him, I quickly snatched the knife from the table. He was thrown out, and once outside he asked for the knife back.

We told him to piss off and laughed at the fool. If he didn't like it, he could always go to the police. Unbelievably he did, and about an hour later three stroppy WPCs turned up, demanding that we hand the knife over as we had committed a theft. And furthermore, if it was not handed over, one of us would be arrested.

We couldn't believe what we were hearing. So they were saying that we should have let the guy walk out with a knife in his pocket? I tried to explain the situation but they were having none of it. They simply didn't want to listen to anything I had to say, and kept demanding the knife be returned immediately.

I didn't have the knife anyway: one of the supervisors from the security company turned up just before the police arrived and so I'd given it to him to take back to the office. The WPCs didn't believe me and gave us twenty-four-hours to return the knife to the police station. If not, they would be back.

The next evening I collected the knife from the office and went to the police station to talk to someone in authority. I wanted to see if I could get someone to make sense of the situation. I spoke to the sergeant on duty, and his attitude was completely different. He thanked me for taking the knife off the guy and assured me that when he turned up to collect it, he would be arrested for carrying an offensive weapon. I suppose we got the right result in the end. If I see him again I think I'll just give him a clump anyway.

New Year's Eve

It hardly seemed possible that a year had passed. It seemed to have flown by. It never bothered me working at this particular time of the year: we always had a good laugh and there was very little serious trouble to deal with. Most people were just pleasantly pissed and happy, and the atmosphere was generally good.

Everyone was having a good time at the night club. The place was decked out with balloons and streamers, and the music was so loud that you could actually see the windows vibrating. Suddenly we got a shout from one of the barmaids that some fella had passed out on the dance area. I went in to find a big fat bloke lying there with his shirt off, flat on his back right in the middle of the dance floor. He was a really big lump and must have been twenty stone or more. I called for Pete to give me a hand.

We managed to drag him part of the way, which wasn't an easy thing to do with the place absolutely heaving. He started to come around and staggered to his feet. He started to get a little aggressive as he realised that he was being thrown out so I give him a good shove towards the door. He stumbled through the door backwards just as Joyce, the manager, was trying to enter. Poor little Joyce was met by his huge arse and was pinned to the wall outside by it. We came to her rescue and Fat Boy wandered off into the middle of the road and went down flat on his back. The drivers must have thought a new mini roundabout had been built. Joyce thought it was amusing, and at the end of the night she bought us all a few drinks. As we were leaving – bearing in mind that this is about five hours later – I noticed a pair of feet sticking out from behind a bank of fruit machines. It was Fatty: he was bedded down for the night, but God knows how he got back in. Joyce beat a hasty retreat, hopped up onto the bar, flipped her legs over, dropped down on the other side of the bar and Fatty was thrown out for the second, and last, time, hopefully. Happy New Year!

***

February '95

It was a cold Friday evening. Pete and I arrived on time as usual, bang on eight, and assumed our positions on either side of the front doors. The head barman came over and asked if he could have a quiet word. I didn't like the looks of this, and I was right. He has some sad news and he told us that Joyce had died the day before whilst she was on holiday. We were gutted by the news as we were only just getting to know her.

She was young, fit and healthy and full of life. How could she be dead? We couldn't believe it. What a terrible loss of a young life. I felt sad about it all and especially so for her young child who was now without her mother.

The last time I'd seen Joyce, she was happy – sitting on the sofa in the bar and singing along to a song with a couple of her friends. That's how I will remember her. God bless.

The place was never quite the same again after Joyce's death, and it definitely went downhill after that. Successions of manager came and went and then a permanent manager was given the licence. Her name was Jo. She was a very attractive young woman with an outgoing personality. She was slim, blonde and in her mid to late-twenties. She was also an ex-copper. She would often take great delight in reminding me that she still had her uniform and handcuffs upstairs, the little devil.

Actually her being ex-old bill was an advantage for us. She would often have a word on our behalf when the police turned up to the occasional altercation, and even when there was more than reasonable force being applied to our attackers. She spoke up for the lads and me many times. I liked Jo; she was very shrewd but quite shy and vulnerable really, a good-hearted person as well. We had a few laughs with her and she would always sort us out with a couple of beers at the end of the night.

Over the next few weeks a number of different guys were sent down to work with us. Paul was one of the new recruits. He was mean-looking with his close-cropped hair and close-shaven beard. He also had a cut running the entire width of his forehead, apparently caused by someone slashing him with a Stanley knife.

I was standing at the door one night and I happened to notice a very well-known male dancer walking past. I had seen him walk past quite a few times on his way to the train station which was nearby. I think he was performing at the theatre just around the corner. He had a big bunch of flowers with him this time and Paul walked over to him and said, "Have you bought those for me?"

Paul frightened the life out of him: he did a quick couple of side-steps and was away. I never saw him again – he must have taken the scenic route and by-passed the club from then on. Paul had that effect on some people.

Paul stayed with us for about six weeks. That was the quietest period I'd ever had at the club; maybe it had something to do with him. We used to get a few old dossers mooching about, and every Friday night, without fail, the same one used to turn up and try to get in. He was a small old Scots guy. He wore a battered old straw trilby hat with tufts of red hair protruding from underneath the brim. He had elastic bands around his shoes to keep the soles on and he was literally on his uppers. As he came closer to me, I could see the dirt and filth on his shirt – well, it wasn't like dirt, it was probably more like topsoil.

"I'm coming in – who's going to stop me?" Hic! Burp! Fart!

I turned and pointed in the direction of Paul.

"He will," I said.

"HIM! He should be in a fucking cage."

He marched up the high street mumbling and shaking his head and I never saw him again.

Paul was asked to take over the door at another venue and he was replaced by a new member of the team: a tall, fair-haired good-looking young fella, with an eye for the ladies. He was called Sean. We had a slight problem with him, though. He was smaller in stature than Pete and I, and so when we had to ask someone to leave, they almost always turned around and vented their anger against him. Which was a big mistake because he could handle himself well, and coupled with his hot temper that made him quite a handful.

And so there were Pete and Sean and I, and it stayed that way for just over a year.

One of the good things about having Sean with us was that he had a motor. Pete and I were used to getting the night bus, that bus was murder – everyone was pissed, belching, farting and fighting… and the blokes were just as bad. There was also a good chance you would be sitting next to the arsehole you had clumped and thrown out earlier that night.

It was a nice cool spring Saturday evening. Everything was quiet and we decided to have a cup of tea. It was Pete's turn to go next door to get our usual free coffee or tea from the burger bar. The manager used to sort us out with free drinks, and towards the end of the evening she would often bring us out something to eat. I'd helped her out one night when she was having some trouble with a couple of young lads who'd decided to start to smash the place up. They did employ a security guard, a young Indian fella, and some nights we spent as much time in the restaurant helping him as we did in the club. He was a nice guy and so we couldn't just stand by and leave him in the shit.

Sean was inside doing an internal patrol I was on the main entrance. Pete arrived back with two coffees and I had my usual cup of strong tea. Pete went in to give Sean a shout, leaving the drinks on the window ledge.

After about three or four minutes there was no sign of either of them. I stood on tiptoes and looked over towards the dance floor. The smoke machine was making it difficult to see clearly but I could just about make out Pete's head moving around: he was pretty tall and stood out above the crowd. There was tension in the air. I knew something was wrong, and I got the feeling things were about to kick off. I left the front door and shoved my way through the crowd, and as I did so I could hear the tell-tale signs of trouble. Glasses and bottles were being smashed and I could hear shouts and high pitched screams above the music.

About twenty feet away, Pete was being confronted by two young fellas who were both armed with beer bottles. He quickly turned and grabbed one guy, dislodged the bottle from his hand and threw him to the floor. Sean was next to him, exchanging punches with some other fella. Sean quickly spun on his heels and delivered a perfectly timed roundhouse kick to the bloke who was about to bounce a bottle off the back of Pete's skull. The well-timed kick connected on the guy's nose and the immediate torrent of blood from his nostrils looked black under the strange lights. Sean then continued to swap punches with the other fella. Just as I got there, he drew back his right hand and sent it smashing into the guy's jaw.

Everything seemed to be in slow motion. I got that familiar tingling sensation in the pit of my stomach, followed by icy cold shots of adrenaline racing through my veins. A pint glass came flying out of the crowd. I ducked just in time and it missed my head by inches. It smashed against the wall in front of me, sending shards of glass into the air. As it exploded, the fragments of glass looked like shimmering snowflakes in the strobe lighting. I didn't see who threw it, but sometimes, when things are kicking off, other people who are unconnected decide to join in for fun.

Sean's right hand punch was now becoming a regular visitor to the guy's face, delivering stinging, painful blows.

This fella was getting a right pasting. He must have received at least half a dozen unanswered punches. I moved in on him and slipped the noose around him. As soon as I locked the hold on, he had no chance. He was game, though, and his right hand was searching for a bottle to use against me. He picked up a beer bottle but with a quick squeeze on his carotid arteries the bottle fell to the floor… he was history.

While dragging him backwards through the crowd, I managed to manoeuvre him over to the main entrance. Sean was right beside me and Pete was now back with us. I turned and faced the door and pushed him outside into the street. Just as I released the hold on him, Sean delivered a perfect right cross which connected on the guy's jaw. The impact sent a thin stream of blood and snot from his mouth and nostrils, which splattered on the wall next to me.

Once we were outside, I could see the damage that had been inflicted on him. One side of his face hadn't been touched, while the other side was damaged past recognition, red and swollen, and one eye was completely shut from Sean's relentless accurate blows. He was a mess and wouldn't be entering any beauty contests for a while. I went into the gents to clean the blood from my jacket. When I'd put the guy into the strangle hold, a fair amount of claret from a bad cut over his eye had leaked out onto my sleeve. Blood is quite a stubborn substance to remove as it's very sticky so it took me a while to clean up.

Ten minutes later I made my way back through the crowd to the front doors to find two police cars and an ambulance on the scene. The three guys who had been fighting were taken to the nearest casualty department. The one that Pete had thrown to the floor had landed heavily on his shoulder, and one of them had a bad nosebleed, courtesy of Sean's boot. The other guy that Sean was dealing with was definitely in need of medical attention. Sean was also taken away, not in the ambulance but in a police car. He was arrested and taken to the nearest cell for the night.

Now where's that cup of tea? I thought.

Blessed are the peacemakers.

We went down to the police station after we closed up to see if they were going to release him, but they refused to let him out. However, the charges were dropped next day and he was released from custody. The thing that saved him was that just before the police arrived, he'd purposely head-butted the wall a couple of times and, in doing so, had put a lump over his eye. He told the police that he'd been struck first and was only defending himself and that he was outnumbered. He was lucky as he'd done one of the guys some real damage.

This is a rough game. Some people do not respond to reason: the only thing they understand is violence and the threat of violence. It's the only thing they seem to respect. It is a sad but absolute fact. That is what happened in this case – the people involved here were a very belligerent group of young men who'd had way too much to drink and would not respond to reason. Instead they decided to use violence against us.

Muppets + drink + drugs + violence = ambulance.

Believe it or not, some people's idea of a good Saturday night out revolves around going to the clubs and pubs to fight; to take on all-comers, including the ultimate test – the doormen. Why? I don't know. I have never understood it. Maybe they have to prove something to themselves, but all I know is that we were prepared to take on anyone if necessary. And that's the way it was. I don't like violence but you can't talk to some people.

Prepared is the key word. I was always ready for them. I trained hard and practised as much as I could, and that was my edge over my attackers. Without the training you are no better than the person you are dealing with. If you are not prepared, you will probably lose.

The more fights you observe or become involved in, the easier fighting becomes. It becomes easier because you can read the signs which give you opportunity to anticipate what's going to happen and then you are able to react accordingly. You react without thought sometimes. It's like the instinctive save by a goalkeeper: he doesn't think about what to do, he just does it.

It is what the Japanese refer to as *mushin*, which means 'no mind'. Like old Musashi says, you must strike from the void. But to get to the stage where you can react correctly without thought takes years of dedicated training, using your whole body as a weapon when delivering your counter-attack. To move and parry your opponent's blow, then return your own devastating crushing blow in one movement. That to me is the essence of karate. If you were to think too much about what you were doing, it wouldn't work.

When you seek it, you cannot find it.

CHAPTER TEN
THE FAIRER SEX

It's not all doom and gloom. We had a few good laughs as well. I used to go to the office at Ealing to collect the wages for the lads on Saturday evenings so I was sometimes a little late arriving at the club.

This particular Saturday had seen the defeat of the South African rugby team at Twickenham. The club was full of rugby supporters of both sides. One of them had decided to bring in off the street the dirtiest old tramp they could find. They sat him in the middle of the dance area where he was given a steady supply of ale. His hair was grey and matted, one side sticking up and the other side as flat as a pancake. He was wearing a vest that had taken on a life all of its own – it was covered in some very dodgy looking stains. He was only a little fella but the jacket he had on was easily four sizes too big and the trousers were pulled right up to his chest. Basically, when he moved, the suit followed a moment later.

He'd got to go. I put my gloves on and I got one of the other doormen to reluctantly help me to escort the old fella outside. As we were dragging him through the crowd, he started to respond to the shouts and jeers from the rugby supporters who were finding the whole scenario quite amusing. He started to struggle, and as we were passing a couple of attractive young women seated by the door, he decided to dig his heels in. A scuffle began and the timing could not have been better: as if on cue his trousers dropped to his ankles. He was bollock naked and he treated the two young women to a full frontal. A loud cheer went up and the whole place erupted into laughter.

We eventually managed to throw him out and watched him as he zig-zagged up the high street still holding a bottle of beer, with trousers at half-mast, singing away without a care in the world. *Brilliant, what a way to start the evening,* I thought.

Another humorous situation occurred with the return of a peculiar woman whom we had barred a couple of weeks earlier. She was very drunk that night and had become really abusive, so she was asked to leave the premises. It was not my fault that as she went through the door she tripped and fell on her fat arse. She thought I'd tripped her up, and started blaming everyone for her embarrassing predicament. She then picked herself up and continued her tirade of foul language in our direction.

She'd fallen over because she was blind drunk. Perhaps I'm a bit old fashioned, but to see a young woman in that state makes a very depressing spectacle. Initially you find it mildly amusing, but when you think about it, it's pretty sad really. Unfortunately it is a common occurrence in this game and dealing with them is all part of the job.

It was getting near to last orders and we still had a small queue at the front doors when this old trout turns up. She walks to straight to the front, much to the annoyance of a big fella who was next in line. She was ranting and raving and demanding to be allowed in. I was called to deal with the situation. I told her she had no chance and to go away, or words to that effect. It was the same woman who was on her arse the previous Saturday.

"Can I go in now, mate?" the fat fella said.

Before I could say a word, she screamed at him like a maniac and told him to fuck off at the top of her voice, and then she took a huge swing at him. He luckily managed to avoid her telegraphed attack. *Here we go, round one,* I thought as the bell for last orders is rung. A red mist must have descended over this normally peaceful creature: he wasn't worried about being attacked by this lunatic, but, because of her, the frightening prospect of not getting in to savour the last few pints of his Saturday night out was becoming a reality.

It was all too much for him and a peach of a right hand punch caught her flush on the chin. Mike Tyson would have been proud of that one. She went down, then got up to stagger down the road, holding her chin. *Not too much to say now,* I thought.

I told fatty off for what he'd done. He was very apologetic and so I let him in to purchase his well-deserved pint.

To the victor the spoils.

Don't get me wrong, I am not condoning violence against a woman at all, but this person wouldn't respond to normal requests. She was ruining everyone's night out and threatening us all at the door. She used so many expletives she actually ran out of them and then tried to use violence because she could not get her own way: just the sort of girl you could bring home to meet your mother.

She was drunk, violent and foul and got what she deserved. The fairer sex? My arse.

Peter, Sean and I were standing outside the front doors. The usual crowds were all filing past when I noticed a young woman walk by. She stopped suddenly, turned around and came back in our direction and then entered the bar. About thirty seconds later, we heard screams and that tell-tale sound of breaking glass. The alarm was sounded and we rushed in to find that the girl who'd just walked in had smashed a pint glass over some guy's head.

Pete was the first one inside and he grabbed the young woman. She was going ballistic, shouting and screaming at some fella who was sitting by the window. Pete put her in the strangle hold – after all, this is the nineties, equality and all that. And so she was thrown out like any other violent person. Male or female, they were all treated the same. As she went past me, I noticed that she had a large cut on her right hand. As she was released from the hold, she sprinted up the road and disappeared. Actually, we should have kept her there in case the guy wanted to press charges, but I'm glad we didn't in the end because he was a right little wanker. Sean was busy throwing the guy who'd been attacked out of the door. He had a couple of nasty cuts to his scalp and blood was trickling down his forehead. He also had some small shards of glass sticking out of the top of his head.

The guy wasn't too happy about being thrown out and tried to go back into the bar. Sean grabbed him by the collar of his shirt from behind and yanked him off the step and back outside. He must have pulled the guy really hard because the whole back of the guy's shirt came away in Sean's hands. It was like something out of a Laurel and Hardy film. He turned around in disbelief and pointed at Sean and said, "You owe me a fucking new shirt, you bastard."

We don't generally respond to well to that kind of behaviour. Sean called him a stupid prick and laughed in his face. The guy was standing outside with pieces of glass in his head, blood trickling down his face and wearing half a shirt, and also the girl he'd been with in the bar had done a runner. I would imagine he'd had better nights out.

What happened was that this fella's regular girlfriend had seen him through the window with another young woman as she walked past. She'd entered the club and smashed a pint pot over his head. He'd taken a swing at her and the rest you know.

Young love, all together now – ahhhhhhh.

Two weeks on

Pete and I turned up as usual one night but Sean had been replaced by the guy who was the regular doorman at that horrible little place down in Chav Town. I thought it was a bit odd, as the office would normally tell me if there were to be any changes. So, we'd got this Kiwi fella and Sean had gone down to Chav Town with Alex and Garry, the two doormen I mentioned earlier.

We'd only been there about half an hour when the alarm went off. As soon as you heard that, you got an instant, massive hit of adrenaline surging through you. Pete and I went in to find two groups of young fellas, about eight or nine of them in total, involved in a mass brawl. Two guys were rolling around on the floor punching, nutting and kicking each other, while the rest of them were engaged in one big scrap where boots and fists were being used in a high speed frantic tangle of bodies. Chris, the Kiwi doorman, had got two of the guys in headlocks and was pulling them towards to exit. Pete and I quickly got to grips with the situation, administering strangle holds all round. We separated the fighters and ejected the ringleaders. I was surprised that there weren't any serious injuries to deal with as they were going for it good style.

As things calmed down I went back to the front door and I noticed that my boots had a splattering of blood across them. We then noticed a thin red trail of blood leading from the front doors of the club. It went along the pavement and up the main street. At the top of the road were a couple of the lads we had thrown out: they were sitting on the pavement and one was holding the side of his head. As I got a bit closer, I could see blood seeping out between his fingers and running down the side of his face and neck. I asked him if I could see the injury, and as he took his hand away I could see that he had been given a Van Gogh – the guy's ear had almost been sliced in two.

He had been slashed with a very sharp knife probably a Stanley knife. We called an ambulance and the wounded soldier was carted off and stitched up and he would live to fight another day, but not in our club. He was lucky, because an inch or two lower and it would have severed an artery. What a nasty violent world we live in.

I was thinking, *I wonder how Sean's getting on.* The two lads he was working with had had some kind of altercation with a pikey (Irish traveller) earlier on and had given him a bit of a slap. They got the usual threat of him coming back to sort them out later on, bla bla bla. Most of the time nothing happens – it's just someone trying to salvage a bit of pride – but you've always got to be ready for the possibility that they will carry out the threat. You've got to stay switched on and it's always a really good idea to have a plan B just in case it all goes tits up.

Every doorman's nightmare suddenly became a brutal reality: the guy came back and he bought a few friends along who decided to bring a claw hammer each. The ten of them proceeded to take the place apart. They smashed everything in the pub, including Garry and Alex. They were beaten to the floor and given the full treatment with hammer and boot. The two lads had a variety of injuries, as you can imagine, and were hospitalised for a while. But they were tough lads and recovered with no lasting problems. Sean survived the affair with little or no injuries. He was lucky. There was something of the inevitable about that: it was just waiting to go off in that place. Sean was back with us the next week but he didn't seem to be his old self. I think he was still suffering from what had happened the week before at Chav Town.

It was getting near to closing time. Last orders had been called and the two lads adopted their usual positions either side of the main doors, which was now a one-way door: out only. I went in to get the punters moving when I noticed that Jo, the manager, seemed to be having a few problems with a couple of guys. I made my way over behind them and overheard Jo tell them that she wanted them to leave.

One of the lads said, "I'm not being thrown out by a barmaid."

"Barmaid? I'm the bloody manager! I don't have to throw you out anyway; I have security to do that for me," Jo replied.

"No poxy doorman's going to throw me out either," he said.

I stepped forward and took over the conversation; I could see where this one was going.

"Put your drink down mate, the manager wants you to leave."

"Fuck off," he said.

He had now also adopted a more aggressive attitude. My kind and courteous manner was being perceived as a weakness and I was rewarded with abuse. Violence being imminent, I took the initiative. Before he started swinging I grabbed his throat with one hand and took hold of his other hand, which contained a pint glass. Sean had made his way over and Pete stayed in position on the front door.

I pushed the lad over to the front doors where Pete put him into a strangle hold. Panic had set in and he'd started to try and slip out of the hold, but once that hold is locked on, you're finished. Pete took over and the guy was sent flying out of the door. As I turned around I was confronted by a mate of his. What we hadn't realized was that there were seven of them, and they were all aggrieved at the fact their friend had been ejected. And so they all decided to converge on yours truly.

The first attacker came forward in a boxing-type pose and started to swing wildly with lefts and rights, aiming them at my head. I threw a hard fast right cross; it was a natural reaction, a strike from the void perhaps. It connected smack on the guy's chin. He did a 360 and spiralled down to the floor and out. I kept moving around with my hands in the ready position; everywhere I looked someone was coming at me.

The next combatant threw a punch at Sean, which missed. Sean was more accurate with his and a hard left hand crunched into the guy's jaw, which sent him stumbling into my direction. A right-hander from me sent him over to Pete who dumped him outside on the pavement.

The next one, a little bigger than the others, adopted some form of fighting stance. He came forward with his fists clenched and decided to also try his luck. Before he had time to think about what he was going to do, I moved slightly to my right and delivered a quick, accurate, powerful open hand strike; it was a technique that I'd practised for years. It went through his guard and the palm of my right hand struck him in the centre of the chest. The impact sent him flying backwards and he went upside down over a table full of drinks sending glasses, bottles and punters in all directions.

Now we had two outside and two on the deck: three to go. When they saw their mate go flying over the table it must have sent the right message. They decided to fight another day. They tiptoed over their fallen comrades and walked out under their own steam.

I would imagine the whole thing was over in less than thirty seconds, but when it's actually happening it seems a hell of a lot longer than that. I took no chances; you can't, especially nowadays. Anyone that presented themselves as a target was treated as one. Remember, the Queensberry rules go out the window. We're going home in one piece and that's all that really matters.

The rest of the evening's revellers were very accommodating, and at closing up time it only took about ten minutes to clear the place. Jo asked if we would like to stay for a few beers, and so, after a great deal of arm-twisting, we were treated to a few well-deserved pints. Sean would almost always have a girl waiting for him and tonight was no exception: his chat up lines seemed to have paid off. We finished our drinks, said goodnight to Jo and jumped into Sean's little motor, which was a bit of struggle at the best of times as it was only a Mini Metro. I let Pete get in first and Sean's date jumped in the back with him. She was a pretty girl but talk about thick; if her brains had been made of dynamite she wouldn't have had enough to blow her hat off. Mind you, I don't think he was too interested in what she had between her ears.

Sean dropped Pete and I back at my place. Wife and kids were in bed hours ago and I'd stocked the fridge with a few beers before I left that evening, so we chilled out with an ice-cold beer, listened to a little of Pink Floyd and mulled over the night's shenanigans.

CHAPTER ELEVEN
REALITY

So, what's it like to have a real fight? Generally there are three stages, and all of them are unpleasant. This is the way I see it.

First stage: Verbal sparring

A short conversation/argument is generally the precursor to a fight, although sometimes your adversary can just start swinging after very little or sometimes no verbal sparring. There's some real nutters out there, don't forget. But that's an exception to the rule, and usually there's always a good amount of a vicious, venomous, verbal exchange. At this stage I would now already be taking up a defensive mind-set and subtly moving my body into my fighting or ready position, and making a note of the guy's hands and getting the distance right. This is the stage where you have an opportunity to try talk them down and calm the situation.

This is also the moment when the fear begins to build inside you. As your attempt at reasoning begins to crumble quicker than the Atlantic ice shelf, the horrible frosty hand of fear starts to run up and down the backs of your shaky legs. This rather unpleasant sensation can sometimes overwhelm you, if you allow it to. Remind yourself that this is the effect of adrenaline: it is all perfectly natural and it is there to help you.

Second stage: Combatives

If attempts at calming the situation by passive methods have failed and all attempts at a spoken reconciliation have now pretty much ended, then this is the beginning of the second stage: the point of no return, the fight itself.

When attacked, I always did roughly the same things:

- I used my surroundings to my advantage
- I always tried to keep my attacker going backwards and off balance
- I kept my fighting stance strong but, at the same time, I was light on my feet.

I aimed to make sure that my first blow was the most telling one. I wanted to take the fight out of the man right from the off. I would wait for the right opening, look straight at the target area and then send out the strike like a guided missile to explode on his chin.

After the first exchange of blows, all feelings of fear completely disappear. I felt nothing, emotionally or physically. A numbness of the mind seemed to take control, a shutting down of all rational thought was in process and a strong sense of survival kicked in.

So here you are, one on one, you and him out in the unforgiving street, going toe to toe. There are no soft mats to land on here, no referees to stop the fight when you go down, and no established rules of fair play.

The senses then suddenly become heightened by a secondary shot of adrenaline. Sometimes you will experience tunnel vision and a slow motion effect begins as your adrenaline courses through your veins. You're now completely alone out there and this really is it: all you've got to rely on is your courage and the skills you have practiced, plus a 'never say die' mind-set. It is essential to prevail at all costs or you'll be going down to the cold hard pavement, and that's one place you definitely don't want to be.

Third stage: Aftermath

Generally these altercations are, thankfully, over quite quickly. I found that one or two solid, accurate shots on the chin were generally sufficient to end the sad spectacle.

I was always quietly confident and believed that I had an advantage over these bar room brawler types. But I also felt that my victories were somewhat hollow. I was never in a celebratory mood afterward. In fact, I must admit that I felt a little ashamed by it all. Even though they were all horrible, nasty, violent creatures who would, if given the opportunity, think nothing of stamping my head into the ground, I still can't say that I ever felt good about defeating them. Even if my actions were considered to be justifiable at the time, it still didn't sit right with me and it always left a bitter taste in my mouth.

So that's my analysis of a violent altercation. Other people may and certainly will feel differently about such things. I know for a fact that some people enjoy the experience and actually seek out violent confrontation.

A lot of people will take an instant dislike to you when you work as a bouncer. There may be many deep rooted reasons for that. Many people don't like the police, whereas I think they do a splendid job... Authoritarian figures are disliked, plain and simple.

If you're a drug dealing scumbag, for example, and you're being prevented from plying your despicable trade by the bouncer, the dealer's not exactly going to put you at the top of his Christmas card list, is he? Bouncers are a necessary evil: we need them. They are our nocturnal guardians, tirelessly weeding out the trouble makers so the decent punters can enjoy a night out without being hassled, bullied, assaulted, robbed or abused.

This is why you sometimes see bouncers engaged in fighting. This weeding out process is where at least seventy-five percent of the trouble starts. So the next time you see a doorman exchanging blows with a punter, think about the reasons why this may be happening, and don't be too quick to jump to conclusions. Believe me, sometimes you really are left with no other choice but to defend yourself.

You've got to be careful, though. You can't go over the top as no one wants to be spending the night in a stinking police cell or suffer the real possibility of a longer stretch. In court you would not be able to put forward the case for 'reasonable force' being applied if you've been trying to score drop goals with the guy's head.

CHAPTER TWELVE
STAND YOUR GROUND

17 March '95: St Patrick's Day

All was going well until I spotted a big fella in the bar in bare feet. He had decided for some reason to take his work boots and socks off and place them on the bar. He was about six feet tall with long frizzy red hair, and was a dead ringer for Mick Hucknell from the pop group Simply Red, but about five stone heavier. He was with about seven or eight of his pals and they were all knocking back copious amounts of the black stuff and getting really loud and overexcited. I asked him very politely to put his boots back on but he refused. *Here we go again*, I thought.

I told him to stop acting like a gobshite. I figured he might get the picture if I spoke to him using some of his own language. He did, although a little reluctantly, and the socks and boots went back on.

I went back to the entrance and left them to it. You've got to be realistic. I knew that you couldn't push your luck too far with Paddies: they can be a most unpredictable sort and liable to start swinging at any moment. It's in their blood, and I should know being half Irish meself.

About ten minutes later, eight or nine other Irish fellas tried to enter the club. They were all pissed as farts and so we had no choice but to knock them back. It was a difficult one as what do you expect any decent, self-respecting Irishman to be doing on a night like this. But this was not the kind of place to be doing it in: this was a night club and not a spit and sawdust piss hole.

As you can imagine, they were not too pleased at being refused entry and decided to give us a lot of nasty verbal and started to crowd the door. Meanwhile, the fella who had his boots off earlier was trying tell us that the guys outside were his mates and they'd behave themselves.

Here we go. You get this lot together and there will be murders. Nine outside, eight inside and we are in the middle, outnumbered as usual. We may have to get the tools out to even up the odds, I thought.

I had a fair idea of what was going to happen here, so Simply Red got a hard shove in the chest and stumbled backward into the bar. I quickly pulled the door shut; luckily it opened outward so I was able to put my foot against the bottom of it to prevent it opening.

Just as I was doing that, one of them jumped up out of the crowd outside and threw a punch over his mate's shoulder and smacked Sean right in the eye. As soon as the blow landed, the three of us burst forwards out of the doorway to engage them all in a mass brawl. Verbal is one thing, but they were now trying to take the door. *Well, if we must have it then let's have it good and proper then,* I thought, as I reached inside my jacket for the bruising irons.

We were up for that one, and I guarantee you that a few of them would have never forgotten that particular St Patrick's day.

At that moment, a passing police van screeched to a halt right outside the club. One of the police officers took a look at Sean's eye which was rapidly swelling and turning into a nice little shiner.

"Do you want to press charges?" the police officer said.

"No, but I want to take him around the corner for a straightener," Sean said.

"I didn't hear that," the policeman said as he walked away.

The guy who had thrown the punch overheard the remark and a scuffle ensued between Sean, this bloke and two coppers. Two other Paddies started to give the old bill some verbal as well and refused to move, and so, with a bit of a struggle, they were all arrested. We managed to get rid of rest of them and the ones who were inside decided to leave as well.

About an hour later, three of them came back to apologise for their friend's behaviour because, apparently, it had nothing to do with them. The older guy, who was a real coffin dodger, said to me that he was a gentleman and didn't want any trouble. He promised to behave if I let him back in the club.

"Bollocks, you've got no chance," I said.

The guy went crazy, and started shouting and screaming.

"I'm going to rip your fecking head off," he yelled, whilst pointing at me.

Stupid old git, you couldn't punch a dent in a pound of butter, I thought. His two companions tried to restrain him but he was having none of it. My patience now exhausted, I decided to give him an opportunity to carry out his threat.

I stepped outside the door and onto the pavement and challenged all three to have a go. I'd had enough of their drunken bravado and bullshit and their tirade of insults. Suddenly their courage had seemed to fail them. They declined my offer of a straightener and beat a hasty retreat back to the Emerald Isle.

We stayed for a while after closing up and we had our usual couple of drinks with Jo, but on this particular occasion we were joined by one of the barmaids. She was a big old sort, about five feet two and weighing in at around the sixteen-stone mark. She had a large backside which, every time she went past, reminded me of a rhino's hindquarters. She'd therefore acquired the unflattering title of 'the big un', and after a couple of drinks she used to always get a bit fruity.

She was wearing an unflattering tight-fitting short skirt and a blouse that must have been a couple of sizes too small; the buttons on it were under an enormous amount of strain trying desperately to contain her huge knockers and rolls of fat. *They'd have someone's eye out if they popped off,* I thought. Pete said that she had touched him up earlier that night. *Fuck me, she must be desperate.* She sat down and joined in the conversation and announced that she had been taking classes in the art of massage. I happened to mention to her that Sean had been complaining of a bad back earlier in the evening, even though he hadn't. She then decided to give a practical demonstration.

Sean's shirt disappeared in a flash: suddenly he found himself half-naked and at the mercy of a sex-starved Sumo in knickers. He was quickly put into a half nelson and placed face down over a table where she now went to work on him. Her strong, chubby digits were prodding, poking and rubbing him all over. She looked over at me while still working on poor old Sean.

"You're next, big boy," she said to me.

I decided that a tactical withdrawal might be a good idea. I was out that door like a fucking rocket.

Sean decided to part company with us. He decided to set up his own customer relations business (that's a joke, by the way). It was something to do with wheel clamping I think and the best of luck to him.

I missed working with him. He'd backed us up without fail every time when things kicked off. He was one of the most fearless guys I know. Like me, he had the mind-set that to go down fighting was preferable to any other option. He was a little crazy sometimes, but also immensely likeable and would always be there right beside you and would get right into the thick of things. He'd be trading blows without much of an invitation.

CHAPTER THIRTEEN
A DESCENT INTO VIOLENCE

May 1995

Our new recruit was a big lad and about twenty years old – a bit too young for this game really, but we would try and look after him. Mind you, he didn't look as if he needed looking after as he was built like a brick shit house. He had a shaven head with tattoos all over the place, but you can't judge by appearances, now can you?

After a few months we were all getting on quite well. Simon was a really likeable guy and was always laughing and joking around. However, he did have a bit of a flaw to his character: he had a really violent temper, which I think might get him into serious trouble one day. I tried to show him the finer points of door etiquette – the diplomatic ways in which you could escort a difficult punter off the premises without resorting to fisticuffs. His way was to engage the transgressor in a very short verbal exchange combined with a head butt between the eyes.

What we have here is a failure to communicate.

The office rang me and asked if Pete and I would look after a club down in Greenford. The boss said that one of the supervisors would run us down there. Halfway through the journey, Steve, the supervisor, said he was glad he hadn't been asked to look after the place as he thought it was a bit dodgy.

"Why? Where are you going, then?" I asked.

"I'm going to look after a pub in the East End later on tonight," he said.

Apparently that pub was a popular underworld haunt. He didn't fancy a night in Greenford, but had no problem working in the East End for some well-known gangsters. He clearly knew something we didn't. I asked him what the SP in Greenford was. Steve told us that the doormen who used to work there were not best pleased in losing their venue and that there was talk of reprisals against anyone who took over the door. Guess what, this was the first night of us new doormen working there.

Fuck 'em, if they try anything they'll come unstuck, I thought

We eventually arrived at the place and Steve didn't hang around, waving to us as he shot out of the car park with wheels spinning and disappearing in a cloud of dust.

It was a big venue with a largely Irish clientele. Two huge front doors led into a porch area, which was where we positioned ourselves for the evening. We had a CCTV monitor just inside the door: it had a quartered split screen, giving us an all-round view of the place. Inside was a long straight bar with six or seven very busy staff rushing about behind it. There was a large stage to the rear, and in front of that about a hundred chairs had been set out.

As the live band was setting up, the manager came out to give us the once-over. I asked him what the previous door staff were like. He said that they were three very arrogant young Asian lads. One in particular would occasionally demonstrate his dexterity with a butterfly knife, spinning it around in his hand in full view of the punters. *Amateurs*, thought I.

One of the barmen was asked by the manager to stay with us and point out any undesirables. He also had to stay there and collect the entrance fee.

The place was starting to fill quite rapidly. Everyone seemed to be in good spirits and all were acting perfectly normally. As the band started to play their first number, some fella got up onto the stage and started crawling about. We went in, and to the cheers of the crowd picked the guy up by his arms and deposited him back into his seat.

It was all very light-hearted and the band started to play on, but two minutes later he was up again, this time trying to give his own rendition of 'My Way'. *He's got to go this time,* I thought, as we dragged him off the stage. There was loud applause as we dumped him outside on the pavement.

He got up off his arse and started to argue a bit and then the manager came over to intervene. He told the guy he could come back in if he agreed to behave himself. I suggested that he let us deal with him; clearly he'd had way too much to drink and was only going to get worse. But the manager said he'd give him one last chance to behave and so he went back in and almost immediately was up on the stage giving an Elvis impression. It was quite amusing, but he was going out for good this time. We dragged him off the stage and threw him outside. I stayed inside the door with the barman and Pete was on the outside, keeping an eye on him as he walked up the road.

"What's that bloke doing now, mate?" I asked.

"He's getting into a rubbish skip."

"You what?"

A few minutes later:

"What's he doing now?" I said

"He's getting out of the skip and he's got a big lump of wood," Pete said

"What's he doing now?"

"He's swinging it around his head and he's coming back towards the pub!"

I didn't see the barman leg it – I just felt the wind as he went past disappearing into the back of the beer garden, some fifty yards away.

As the guy got closer to the venue I went out to face him while Pete moved off to one side. He looked at me and then at Pete – we were now on either side of him. We got a closer look at the lump of wood he had taken out of the skip: it was a four foot piece of three by two with two or three large crooked nails sticking out of one end.

Nasty little bastard, I thought.

He had it in a two-handed baseball bat grip. But before he had time to think about who he was going to whack first, I moved forward, which distracted him for a second. Pete then quickly nipped in from the side and snatched the weapon out of his hands. The longer the delay in this type of scenario, the worse it becomes. The aggressor will begin to gain in confidence, so always move in hard and fast. Ordinarily, in this type of dangerous confrontation, once we'd disarmed him we would have given him a right pasting, but he was a pretty pathetic character so all he got was a hard slap across the chops and boot up the arse from Pete.

We also let him know that if he came anywhere near the place again tonight that he would most definitely be feeling the worse for wear in the morning. I looked at my watch: we had only been at the place an hour.

There were no more incidents that night. It turned out to be one of the best nights that we'd ever done. The bar staff supplied a steady supply of soft drinks (we never had more than two halves of lager each whilst we were working on the door). After yes, during no: that was part of our unwritten code. The band dedicated their last number to the two lads on the door. It was called Black Velvet; the very attractive lead singer did an excellent rendition. She was looking at me all through the song – well, that's what I told Pete anyway. We were paid some very fine compliments that night by staff and punters who thought we had done a very professional job.

All that stuff about the previous doormen coming back to sort us out? Well, that was the usual load of old bollocks.

The next venue we were going to look after was a large place in Ealing, which was a large very busy bar by the green. There were four or sometimes five of us on that door. We'd worked there before a couple of times so we knew the routine.

Pete and I worked inside and let the regular team sort out the front. They knew all the faces that weren't welcome. There wouldn't have been much point us being on the front doors as we might have let in punters who'd been barred.

There was one large staircase where one of us would stand and the other one would be positioned above at some distance, away on a high balcony which overlooked the whole of the ground floor area. Communication was the problem in this place as the deafening music put the block on using radios so we acquired a small flashlight each and worked out a couple of signals. Two flashes stood for assistance needed: keeping it simple was the name of the game.

I was standing on the large staircase, my feet being at head height of the customers sitting below me. I suddenly felt a hand slowly creeping up the inside of my trouser leg. I was a bit worried about looking down. *I just hope that's a woman's hand*, I thought, as there are some very funny people about, you know. I looked down and was relieved to see a very pretty young woman attached to the other end. She was a regular from the other club having a bit of laugh with her mates.

We only had one idiot to deal with. This guy decided that he didn't want to leave at closing time and that he was going to finish the two pints he had left. And there was no way he was leaving before he had done so. We left him to it, hoping that he'd get the message as the place emptied. We had the place cleared, apart from the arsehole who by now was just starting on his second pint. He'd totally disregarded the polite manner in which we'd asked him to leave. *I've had enough of this – we'll be here all night with this bloke*, I thought as I approached him once more. I asked him one last time to put his drink down and leave the premises.

"Fuck off, I'm finishing my drink."

An attitude adjustment was immediately required and this is my way of achieving it. As soon as someone responds like that, as far as I'm concerned he leaves me with very little choice: a left handed slap down and grab onto his right wrist with an immediate right-handed grip onto the throat. Now I have control. You have to do it really quick and with power, otherwise you'll lose the initial momentum. This guy was a big lad, about six two and roughly fifteen stone, but once you have the momentum going, it's not too difficult to get them were you want them to go. Pushing him backward towards the exit with Pete going in front to open the doors, we managed, with a bit of a struggle, to throw him outside. We passed the manager who was looking a little concerned at what was happening.

"That was a bit rough," the young podgy manager said as I came back in.

"I'm sorry, but I wouldn't dream of telling you how to pour a pint beer, now would I?" I said.

It wasn't rough at all, although to the untrained eye it may have seemed so. It was actually a very controlled exhibition of a perfectly executed ejection technique.

Look, at the end of the day, the guy was drunk and was just starting to get a little aggressive. Who knows, that last pint he wanted to finish may have been enough to tip him over the edge and become violent. You can't have the punter dictating to you: aren't we supposed to be giving zee orders around here? I dealt with him before it got nasty and he was thrown out suffering an injury only to his pride. My guess is that the manager was probably fairly new to this game and had rarely seen a punter being treated in this manner.

As we were leaving, the guy who'd been thrown out was waiting outside with his mate and engaged us with a few choice words as we went by. I'd heard it all before and decided to ignore it. They were just a pair of pissed-up pricks looking for trouble – young men who got their courage from the bottom of a beer glass.

As we walked, Pete noticed that they had begun to follow us.

"Ok, Pete we'll go this way across the green and head into the dark. If they want to have a go, we'll choose when and where," I said.

We took a slight detour and led them unsuspectingly into the middle of the green. They continued to follow and were still shouting abuse. They were getting braver and braver as they got closer. We slowed our pace down a little and then came to a sudden halt in a nice dark area.

They were now close behind us and walked straight into the trap – and into the shit.

We allowed them to get a little closer and then turned and confronted our pursuers. They were surprised to see us turn around and face them, turning the tables as it were. The hunters now becoming the hunted. The fear had visibly gripped them.

I gave the guy who had all the mouth a hard shove into the chest. Pete challenged the other guy, who ran away, leaving his mate alone.

The shove in the chest was intended to do two things: the first was to get him to launch his attack there by suckering him into a powerful back kick to the stomach, which he definitely deserved after the amount of abuse and threats he was dishing out. The push away also gave me the right distance to execute the technique which I had practised a thousand times in the little gym; it's an extremely effective strike and a definite finisher when done correctly. Fortunately for him, I didn't have to use it. His bottle went completely and he backed off and decided to run, shouting as he went that if we touched him he would go to the police.

This type of altercation is a prime example of the weekend warrior mentality. When it came down to it, he knew that all he could do was talk like a hard man. You have to be ready though: encounters with these types of characters can be very unpredictable and sometimes your challenge will be accepted. Remember, never underestimate anyone. I had a feeling that I might run into these two fellas again one day.

Pete and I were back at our usual venue the next week. We had decided that we were only going to work here from now on as our particular way of working was not being appreciated elsewhere.

Jo, the manager, was really pleased, if not relieved, to see our return. Absence makes the heart grow fonder, so they say, and I think she was quite fond of yours truly. She told me that there had been trouble at the club during the past couple of weeks and she was more than a bit concerned with what was happening. She told me that she wasn't impressed with Simon's unique brand of door supervising. He had adopted the 'nut first and ask questions later' technique.

I had to admit there were a few undesirable characters in the club and definitely some that I had barred in the past. It was time for a bit of scumbag cleansing.

One guy was a dealer that I'd barred two years ago. He must have been waiting for me to have a night off so he could practice his trade again. He was a strange character, black and of medium build, and he looked like he was trapped in a 1970s time warp. He wore flared trousers and a large brimmed hat, plus shades, of course. I remembered a while back he tried all kinds of variations on what he was wearing to gain access to his once fertile and lucrative market place. It was all part of his false persona – it was all a front to ingratiate himself. He tried to act and look cool and therefore trick the young, gullible punters into thinking that what he was selling was cool as well. He was very compliant though and left immediately: he knew we were not going to fuck around with him.

I have no time for drug dealers. They are near the lowest of the low, right down there with the absolute dregs of society as far as I'm concerned.

An hour later, Jo came out to the front doors and informed us that a new dealer had been spotted on the premises. She said that someone from the drugs squad was coming down to have a word with him. I think he was the other dealer's mate and they were working as a team. However, a bit later Jo got a call from the drugs squad saying that they were too busy and would pick him up another time, but meanwhile they wanted us to leave him alone and we were not to touch him. *Yeah right,* I thought.

Pete and I looked at each other and, without a word, made our way over to our friendly neighbourhood drug dealer. He was a small, thin black guy with shoulder length dreadlocks, which contained a variety of small coloured beads. He wasn't alone and he had three associates with him: two large black fellas, who were both about the same size as me, and a young cocky white guy who thought he was the daddy.

We waited for the right moment and then managed to separate the dealer from his companions. We shoved him into the gents' toilets where we told him that he was leaving. He was more than a little nervous now that he had been separated from his minders. He was visibly shaking as Pete put his size twelve boot to the bottom of the door to stop anyone coming in. I purposely put the frighteners on him. He seemed to think we were going to give him a kicking, I don't know why. Perhaps it was the way I was squeezing his throat that gave him the idea. But we didn't touch him: we figured that he knew we weren't pissing around. All we wanted to do was to get the scumbags out of our club. I pushed him over to the urinal trough and told him that we didn't want shit like him on the premises.

He agreed, but on leaving the gents he quickly darted over to his mates. I was right behind him. I thought he might seek the sanctuary of his friends. After all, how can you trust the word of a drug dealer?

He didn't quite make it. I grabbed him around the neck from behind with one arm and with the other I took hold of his dreadlocks, yanked his feet off the floor and dragged him backwards through the crowd. I threw him out and down onto the pavement. His mates were following right behind, trying to rescue him, and Pete was pushing and shoving them out of the main exit.

All of them had been ejected and were now giving it big style outside. They were all making that sucking of the teeth noise and gesturing with their hands, mimicking the using of pistols. Threats of reprisals were coming thick and fast, mainly from the younger white lad. Apparently he was going to go home and come back to shoot us all later on. After about five minutes, I started to lose it. I'd had enough of the bullshit. With fists clenched I stepped outside and confronted them. *Shit or bust, let's have some,* I thought. Now they had the opportunity to carry out their threats as I walked right up to them.

"Come on then, let's fucking have some!" I roared.

I wanted one of them to make a forward move, but as in most of these types of incidents, when it came down to it none of them decided to accept my offer. They were all mouth and no bottle. They all backed down and walked away.

I shouldn't have gone outside: they had brought me down to their level and I acted out of anger and frustration. I behaved like a fucking amateur and I could have got myself nicked as I was ready to lay into them – with the tools, if necessary. Our job was done and they were outside so there was no need to get involved any further. I think the job was definitely getting to me as my tolerance barriers were becoming far too easy to breach. I must admit, I really wanted to take them on. As I walked out of the door of the club, I wasn't aware of anything. The other lads, as far as I was concerned, had disappeared. I just had one thought: steam straight in. Crazy.

We had a quick drink with Jo at the end of the night, and as usual stood outside and waited as she bolted and locked the doors. Just as we were about to get into the motor, which was parked right opposite the club, we heard someone shouting in our direction. I looked across the road and thought it was the drug dealer and his mates coming back for tear up, but no, it was someone else shouting some form of abuse at Pete. He thought it was someone he'd barred a while back. This guy was a young stocky black lad of no more than twenty. Basically he was showing off in front of a large group of his pals, shouting at the top of his voice.

"Hey, shut the fuck up," I said.

He told me to come and shut him up and started waving his hands. Such arrogance can only be rewarded in one way and his challenge was duly accepted. Pete could see what was going to happen.

"Just ignore it. Let's get in the motor," Pete said

I ignored Pete's sound advice. There was more abuse coupled with sarcastic laughter. I wasn't on the door now; we were on our way home. I was tired and pissed off and I had a splitting headache. Normally I would have made a mental note of the twat and dealt with him another time, but not tonight, I wasn't fucking having it. *Who does he think he is?* I thought.

Within seconds I was marching across the road, adrenaline pumping in my veins and eyes locked on, ready to do battle with our tormentor. As I approached, he started to move about giving a pathetic little Muhammad Ali impersonation. He was smiling and taunting me as he danced about. He seemed to think it was all a big joke and that nothing was going to happen. I didn't say anything but quickened my stride, closed the gap, measured the distance and let fly. I clumped him really hard.

A powerful right hook smashed into the side of the guy's thick skull. As I threw the punch, he'd leant forward a fraction in an effort to duck out of the way and so my blow didn't find its correct target area. It was still a powerful blow, though, and it actually upended him. One second I saw his head, and the next thing I saw was his two feet in the air as he went upside-down and landed flat on his back on the pavement. *Who's laughing now?* I thought, as the collective groan from the small crowd echoed along the high street. The blow had broken one of knuckles in my right hand which was starting to swell: it didn't matter, I still had my left.

The guy was dazed and was still on his back as Simon came running over. He decided to give his own rendition of River Dance on the guy's head, stamping repeatedly on his nose. I stopped him after two or three stamps as he was looking as if he was enjoying it a bit too much.

Then one of his pals decided to help his fallen comrade and stepped in. Simon dealt with him by literally kicking his arse up and down the high street. The busy traffic had come to a halt in the middle of the road to view the spectacle. A double decker bus pulled up and the driver stuck his head out of the window to have ago at us. I walked over and told him to mind his own fucking business. The way we were carrying on, he was lucky I didn't drag him out of his cab. He got the message and fucked off sharpish. I think there must have been a full moon out that night or something. Mad stuff.

Pete decided to call it a day. He said that he'd had enough. I had noticed a few signs of disinterest for a while. He wasn't training as much as he used to either, so it came as no surprise really. He suggested that we both turn it in.

We'd started on this road together and so it would have been appropriate to finish at the same time as well, but I decided to stay on.

What can I say about Pete? His friendship and loyalty were greatly appreciated. It takes a considerable amount of courage to do this job, especially the way that we did it. I always knew that without a doubt he would be there right behind me, watching my back. We always got on well; I don't think we've ever had a disagreement in all the years I've known him. He could be very witty at times as well, which always helped during the more stressful moments.

The scars you acquire while exercising courage will never make you feel inferior. D.A. Battista.

CHAPTER FOURTEEN
STRANGE DAYS

We now move on in time to March 1996

I had the weekend off from the door work as a good friend of mine was having a birthday party at a local pub. I needed a break because sometimes I felt that trouble seemed to be shadowing me and was a constant companion. So a night off from all the trials and tribulations of the nightclub would do me good. I was now the punter for a change.

I'd been in the pub before as it wasn't that far from where I lived. It had always been a rough pub and had a bit of a reputation for attracting the wrong kind of crowd. As soon as we entered the bar, I automatically felt the essence of bad vibes forming. They had a small disco going in the back, which at first was quite good. The only problem was the DJ – he was a real mouthy twat. We'd had words earlier on that evening as he walked by us all at the bar. He'd said something stupid and I reacted. To me he seemed to have far too much to say for himself. He had got a little too familiar and I didn't even really know the fat twat. *We'll see how much you've got to say later on when I come back,* I thought. And a little later on, after we'd all gone home, I jumped into the motor and went back to the pub alone to see what his fucking problem was.

I was a bit pissed that night, but it didn't matter because, in my mind, I desperately needed to have a word with this guy. When I got there the place was empty, apart from some bar staff who were tidying up behind the bar. I strode in like John Wayne and asked one of them where the DJ was. Out of the corner of my eye I suddenly see the big fat lump coming up behind me. I didn't give him an opportunity to Jap me with a sneaky attack from behind. I knew he wasn't coming over to shake my hand so I quickly spun around and clouted him with a right hook, which knocked him out. Now he was a big fella, probably about eighteen stone, and as he went down he clattered into the chairs and tables behind him and scattered them all over place. It was stupid really, looking back: I didn't need to prove myself, I know what I'm capable of and I could have taken that fella with one arm and blindfolded. Still, what's done is done and can't be undone.

A week later I heard that there were a few faces making inquiries as to who I was and there was the inevitable talk of reprisals. I'm not the kind of person to let the grass grow under my feet so I went back into the pub one day on my own. I stood at the bar, stone cold sober this time, and ordered a pint. I'd spotted a small group of dodgy characters in the corner playing cards who eyeballed me as I strolled in. I vaguely knew the governor of the place and when he saw me he came over and I apologised to him for the punch up. He was a friendly guy and an ex-copper I believe. He said that he wasn't surprised that someone had given the bloke a slap as he'd had a few run-ins with him himself. I didn't even get barred for that one. As I said, trouble did seem to follow me around a bit back then, but, on the other hand, maybe the trouble was with me?

***

I was back on the door the following week, back where I belonged. I had yet another new member of the team to indoctrinate. He was a nice guy but, like his mate Simon, was as green as grass and he didn't have a bloody clue. He was quite small in stature but relatively confident. He was in his mid to late twenties and seemed to be able to act as a calming influence over Simon, which was not a bad thing.

Later that night, the two guys with whom I'd had a run in with at the club in Ealing turned up in the queue. They were a bit taken aback to see me and a little apprehensive, to say the least. They both apologised and promised to behave themselves. I let them in, as inside I knew that it would not be long before these two tossers caused some sort of trouble which would then give us a legitimate opportunity to give them a couple of well deserved, well overdue slaps.

We didn't have to wait long: the two bully boys soon started on a couple of younger lads who were just having a quiet night out with their girlfriends. They were both small guys, and one of them was really skinny; I'd seen more fat on a jockeys whip. The two couples left the club, closely followed by our two brave hard men. The fight began outside the club. There was a brief verbal exchange and then the two smaller guys began taking a hammering.

One of them was being repeatedly punched and kicked all over the place. By now the fight had moved away from the club and was continuing outside a lovely little Mexican restaurant about thirty feet away. Tables, chairs and plants were all being knocked about as the mindless assault continued.

The two young women who were with them were hysterically shouting and screaming in our direction and gesturing for our assistance. One of the young lads went down on his back. The two attackers now took full advantage and took turns to stamp and kick the poor guy in the head. Now these two were quite big men and were giving the guy on the deck powerful boots to the head. The guy was now out cold and helpless. We could hear the sound of the boots going in from where we were standing. Two more sickening powerful kicks were slammed into the side of his lifeless head.

Simon and his mate were like a couple of pit bulls straining at the leash in anger at what they were watching. They turned to me and asked if we should get stuck into them. Usually we didn't involve ourselves in what was going on outside as we were there to look after the club and the people inside it. But there are exceptions to the rule.

I unleashed the two lads and they set about mauling the bigger of the two the attackers with all sorts of dirty tricks. Simon initiated the rescue by smashing his forehead into the guy's nose. I grabbed the other one and give him two powerful knee strikes into the stomach; he doubled over and got a right hook to the jaw. Which was enough to end the assault.

"I don't want to fight you, mate," he cried as he went down to the pavement. He curled himself up into a ball so I couldn't get a clean shot at him. *Not so brave now,* I thought.

I called the two lads back in. Simon and his mate had done the other bloke up like a kipper – his eye and nose were pouring with claret from the expert use of Simon's forehead. I didn't know what would have happened if we hadn't moved in to put an end the attack. How many kicks to the head does it take before a fatality occurs?

I got home late that night and sat in the living room alone and thought over the night's antics while sipping an ice-cold beer before crawling up to bed. It was 3am and I was knackered. I took off my boots and carried them up the stairs with me. Half-way up my staircase is a large window that overlooks the front garden and the road. As I passed the window, I saw the headlights of a car as it pulled up right outside my gate. I poked my finger through one of the slats on the Venetian blind and, to my absolute horror, I saw a police patrol car with two coppers inside it. My heart sank into the depths of despair – that feeling of dread before you're about to be nicked is one of the most sickening feelings you can experience.

I turned around and crept back downstairs. As I reached the bottom, I grabbed my jacket and reluctantly slipped my boots back on. All sorts of things were going through my mind. *I bet it's got something to do with those two twats we clumped earlier. Do I deny it? Yeah, best bet is to say nothing at first,* I thought as I waited for the knock of doom.

I waited by the front door with my hands out ready for them to clap me in irons. *Something's not right here, it's taking too long,* I thought. I turned out the light and crept back up to the window and peeked outside. My heart jumped back into place as the police got out of the car and arrested the guy over the road. Yabba dabba fucking doo, I was free again!

The next night we had a little more trouble with a couple of guys who wouldn't do as they were asked. Three times I asked them if they wouldn't mind taking their feet off the seats. Every time my back was turned, they put them back up again. Fourth time now and I'd had enough. These boys were most definitely looking for trouble.

"Ok fellas, you two are leaving," I said.

One of them still had his feet up on one of the cast iron stools.

"We're not going anywhere," he said.

I quickly whipped the stool out from under his feet and he jumped up and immediately adopted a fighting pose. His friend did likewise. He then beckoned me forward.

"Come on, come on then," he said

So I did and I delivered a hard front kick to his knackers. He stopped talking and fell on the floor, clutching his privates. Then, to my surprise, Simon burst through the door and took the other guy out and down to the floor with a very graceful dive, at the same time putting him into some form of mysterious head lock. *He's got to stop watching that American wrestling*, I thought.

We managed to drag them outside and they decided to make a stand. The smaller of the two made a lunge at Simon and was put to the ground, where he received half a dozen blows from Simon's sovereign-encrusted fist into his face.

His companion decided to whip off his belt, which had a very heavy-looking oval-shaped brass buckle attached to it. He proceeded to advance in my direction, swinging the belt around his head. I stayed just inside the doorway where his weapon of choice would have little effect.

All the time that this was happening, I was thinking about the police pulling up outside my house the previous night. I really didn't fancy getting nicked, and that kind of put me in a different frame of mind. I held back this time. They were now really fired up and making all kinds of threats. What they actually said repeatedly was that this was their manor and they would be back tomorrow to settle the matter. These types of encounters will expose your every weakness if you allow them to. You have to fight against all the negative thoughts, stand your ground and *show no fear*.

The warnings and threats were all said in a very calm and deliberate fashion and my life was threatened in no uncertain circumstances. It's a funny feeling someone telling you that they are going to kill you, but you sort of get used to it.

"I'll be here. See you tomorrow, then," I said.

Their parting shot was to throw one of the heavy signboards in our direction, which was ironically advertising the happy hour. It crashed into the door and cracked the side window. Jo was not too happy, and I couldn't say that I was either. In actual fact, the more I thought about these two mugs, the more enraged I was becoming. That was the lowest I have ever felt whilst working on the doors. If I had a pound for every time someone had threatened to shoot me, I'd be a very rich man. Why should I think this time would be any different from all the others? I don't know: perhaps I was becoming paranoid or maybe it was because Sean and Pete weren't around anymore? I'll not back down, I can't, I won't and I'll be here tomorrow so we'd see what they are made of.

They were a couple of nasty characters. I was taking their threats seriously and decided that I might have to introduce them to a couple of friends of mine – 'the bruising irons', as they were affectionately known.

After you have worked in a certain place for a while, especially in this type of occupation, you seem to acquire an amount of territorial pride, as I call it. Perhaps it's wrong to think in these terms, but nevertheless you do, and so that's one reason why some people may stand their ground in these situations. But I think it could simply come down to what kind of person you are inside. Some people refuse to be intimidated and decide to fight back.

My days of allowing someone to intimidate me were over years ago. However, that doesn't mean to say that you don't get a little scared every now and again. It doesn't matter how tough you are, it's natural.

***

It had been raining for most of the day and it was steadily getting worse by the evening. Outside it was black, cold, damp and miserable. I went through a series of strenuous karate exercises before I left home that night and psyched myself up for the potential battle. I got into my old Ford Sierra and drove through the wet streets at a slow, sedate pace thinking of what the night could possibly bring.

I wouldn't say that I was feeling scared: if I had been, I would have stayed at home, I think my mind was quite clear and calm, but I was definitely feeling a little uneasy. What if these two actually turned up? I'd have to live with the consequences of my actions if it all went pear-shaped. Were they a couple of bullshitters or were they up for it? At the end of the day, they were the ones who threatened me and so whatever fate befell them would be of their own making.

I parked the car in the multi-storey car park which was a few minutes' walk away from the club. I knew the guy in the security box at the car park so he used to let me park there for free, which was handy because there was absolutely nowhere to park in that area. I never parked in the same place twice, and I would also vary my times of arrival as well. You've got to stay one jump ahead of your potential ambushers, and if you stay in this line of work for any length of time you will make quite a few enemies.

I would sometimes sit in the car for a good five minutes to watch and wait for a while before deciding to get out. I always reversed the car into the parking space as well, so if I ever had to make a quick getaway it would be much easier if the car was facing in the right direction. Jump in and just put your foot down and you're away. Why make it easy for them? It may sound a bit strange or possibly bordering on paranoia to go through such precautions. Well, I am here to tell my story. I know of at least two people who are no longer around and there are many others. Maybe if they had varied their routine a little, they would still be alive… it's called survival.

I left the car park and approached the club. I decided to go in through the beer garden, which had tall surrounding walls and a high wooden gate which was always locked. When no one was looking I jumped over the top and climbed down into the beer garden, and now I could enter the club through the back of the conservatory. The reason being was that the fellas who were coming back to sort me out could already be inside, possibly turning up before the lads had arrived on the front doors as the small bar was open to the public during the day. The door to the conservatory wasn't locked: it never was. It was a little stiff though and so you had to give it a good shove in the right place to get it to open. I opened the door and entered the club unseen. The place was virtually empty.

About ten minutes later the other two lads arrived and I asked them to work inside tonight. I explained that I wanted to be on the front door all night. They thought it was a little strange but they knew it must have been for a good reason and did as I asked. I didn't want to get them involved in this one, so I told them nothing. What they didn't know couldn't hurt them.

The rain was still falling, adding to the already unpleasant nature of the evening. I wore a three-quarter length waterproof coat for obvious reasons, and also for concealment purposes. I must have looked like Blakey from *On The Buses*. The body armour was on and the bruising irons were in place. Now it was just a matter of waiting and staying switched on. Cold and wet, I didn't move. I stayed put in a position that gave a good all-round view for any attempted attack upon me. My adrenaline was now pumping good style: I was ready.

I hardly acknowledged the people rushing along through the rain. I was concentrating on looking out for my would-be assailants. I never forgot a face, so as soon as they appeared I'd take the fight to them, bash them up and disappear…

I was there for five hours that night and they decided not to show.

The art of war is simple enough. Find out where your enemy is.
Get him as soon as you can.
Strike him as hard as you can and as often as you can.
— Ulysses S Grant

I feel that at this particular time it was becoming easier to settle problems with violence or to resolve the arguments I had on the door with a right-hander, and I wasn't too bothered about it either. You have got to be able to switch into Mr Nasty, and then just as quickly switch him off. I was finding it increasingly difficult to switch him off: the job does that to you after a while.

I was in danger of becoming the same as the violent idiots that I had been fighting against.

I didn't really need the job any more – my wife had gone back to work ages ago and I still had my day job, so why was I still here? I'd got nothing to stay for really. Was it through some form of misplaced loyalty? To whom? I didn't know. So what was it then? Was it a bit of a power trip? I was the head doorman; the lads would carry out my instructions without question. If I said someone was not coming in then that was that, absolutely no argument about it. If I said someone was leaving, out they would go, one way or the other. The camaraderie was another thing. Sometimes it was like a night out with a few pals and it didn't seem like I was at work. So there were aspects of the job which are agreeable. The nightlife, the lively music scene and the regular punters who were genuinely pleased to see you felt good sometimes. I didn't really have a clear answer but I knew it wouldn't be long before I turned it in though.

CHAPTER FIFTEEN
END GAME

A few months on

This weekend was to be my last. I had a feeling there was going to be a few problems. I don't know why, but after a while it seems you can sense the *negative vibes* in the air.

The club was full of Welsh rugby supporters and they had all made the long journey down to London to watch their team take on the English at Twickenham. I'd only been there half an hour or so and my instincts were proved right. I noticed that three lads were involved in a bit of a scuffle at the bar, which was five deep with thirsty rugby supporters. The negativity came in the shape of a local hard man. I had seen the guy before: he fancied himself as a bit of a hard nut and I remembered that he'd had a bit of an attitude problem the last time he was here.

I went in with Simon and calmed the situation. This guy was six two, wide shouldered and lean and mean. He'd had been involved in some sort of altercation earlier on before I arrived so I just gave him and his two mates the benefit of the doubt.

We went back to the front doors while still keeping the occasional eye on the three troublemakers. As I looked over towards the bar area, the taller of the three gave one of the rugby supporters a punch in the side of the jaw. He went down on the floor then scrambled up to his feet and ran outside. Who did this geezer think he was? Once again Simon and I went in, leaving the other two lads on the front doors, but it was a different attitude from us this time.

"You three are leaving," I told them.

They ignored what I said, or they may not have heard me say it, owing to the noise.

Then the tallest one of the three punched another guy who was standing at the bar waiting to be served, right in front of us. *This bloke's a bit of a nutter,* I thought to myself. He was an arrogant drunk, a big bloke who was used to throwing his weight around. That old familiar adrenaline rush was making its presence felt. By now I knew how and, more importantly, when to use it. We both stepped in and a scuffle began. The guy had a face full of scars which told me that he'd probably had a fight or two. *Well, so have I and I'm better at it than you,* I thought and I knew exactly what was going to happen. He'd had the friendly warning: this time we were going straight to stage two.

He quickly turned around and all the signs indicated that he was about to throw his tried and tested right hand punch. After a few of these types of confrontations, you can sometimes anticipate what is about to happen which affords you the opportunity to try and counter your attacker.

I'd just seen him throw two right handers, so my guess was he'd be throwing another one, but you have to look for the signs: that's where your training comes in. His predictability was his downfall. His shoulder moved back slightly and he cocked his right hand. He also carried his left real low. I moved off quickly to the right, away from his right hander which was now on its way. I smashed him with a right cross. The blow knocked him backward and he stumbled back four or five feet and crashed into a table and then onto the deck. He picked himself up out of the debris and groggily stood his ground. I then remembered something that Sean had told me when he was in a similar situation: to get the guy out of the place he rolled up the guy's jacket and threw it toward the door to get him moving. I did the same. I grabbed the guy's leather jacket from the back of the bar stool, rolled it up and threw it over toward the door. It didn't work as he was too dazed to see the bloody thing as it flew past.

I said to Simon to get him around the neck and take him outside, but he couldn't manage it, the problem being that when the guy stood up straight he was too tall for Simon to get a good hold on him. I didn't want to move forward because I'd got his two mates either side of me and they were biding their time. I had them both in my peripheral vision and I knew that the moment my back was turned they'd attack me. It was a bit of a balls up. *Where are the other two lads?* I thought

My guess was that they couldn't see what was going on due to the crowds, and we didn't have any radio communication. For the moment they were deaf and blind to the situation. Meanwhile Simon and this fella become engaged in a scuffle. Simon was actually pretty useless if you took away his ability to nut someone. He didn't have a clue, so against my better judgement I decided to go in and give him a hand. I had an idea what was going to happen so I was ready for them. As soon as I went forward, one of them jumped on my back.

I began to lose all rational thought, and as the guy started to strangle me I slipped into fight mode. These guys had clearly arrived here with one thing on their minds: trouble. They thought they could come here to bully, frighten and intimidate. They'd probably done it before in other clubs and pubs and had gotten away with it. *Well, tonight there're all gonna be on the receiving end for a change.*

I grabbed the guy's arm which was crushing my neck; I twisted, dropped my shoulder, leant forward and executed a really good judo throw on him. He went right over my shoulder, and for a moment I thought he was going through the huge window that overlooked the street.

Luckily he landed on a table with crash, scattering and smashing the bottles and glasses as he landed. He must have knocked himself out as he hit the table because I didn't see him get up. The thick wall of punters' bodies was blocking the access to the front doors and I was left on my own. This was all happening extremely fast, you understand, and only about ten seconds had passed since I clouted the tall fella.

The other guy decided to have ago and he also jumped on my back and started to strangle me. He was quite strong and wasn't doing a bad job either. He had a really good grip around my neck and he was slowly choking me out. I was becoming light-headed and my vision was starting to fade out. I started to stagger around like Frankenstein's monster. This little shit was attached to me like a fucking limpet and in a matter of seconds I'd be going down and out on the floor. I managed to force my hand up the inside the crook of his elbow and grab the sleeve of his jacket. I then had some purchase and managed to swing him around violently, which thankfully dislodged him from my back. He was now right in front of me. I quickly stepped in and delivered a hard jolting left upper cut under his jaw. *Yeah, 'ave some that,* I thought.

It was an excellent punch; you know when you have delivered one just right because you don't even feel it. You only see the impact. I grabbed him by the hair to hold him still. My fingers were now clamped tight around his greasy locks and I gave him two more short sharp left hooks on the chin. I let go of his hair and he fell to the floor unconscious, where he got the order of the boot. Actually, I think the first punch had knocked him out and it was only because I was holding him by his hair that he'd remained upright. One of the other lads finally pushed his way through the crowd and he dragged the fella along the floor and out toward the doors. The whole thing had lasted no more than thirty seconds.

I didn't have a clue what else had been happening, but as I started to regain some form of normality I moved toward the front doors where I heard some hysterical screaming. It was coming from one of the young barmaids. She was looking down at the floor where a crowd had now gathered. I pushed my way through and saw the guy who Simon was scuffling with earlier lying flat on his back.

The guy was unconscious and his face was covered in thick gooey blood. I knelt down beside him and I could hear that his breathing was very shallow and he was gurgling with each breath. The music suddenly went off and the lights came on. Under the bright white lights his face presented a horrible spectacle: it was just a red mask. His lips were turning blue: I had to do something and fast. I was on my own and it was down to me save the guy, as the punters were standing and staring wide-eyed in shock. The blood from his injuries had run down into the back of his throat and it was slowly choking him to death. I suddenly remembered what to do and some basic first aid kicked in. *A B C – airway, breathing and circulation,* I kept repeating to myself.

I turned the lanky lump on his side into the recovery position, firstly checking that he hadn't swallowed his tongue. I then took hold of his head to put it into position but it was so slippery with all the blood that it slipped from my hands and banged into the hard wooden floor with a sickening thud. I tried again and this time I managed to get him into the recovery position. Thankfully that seemed to do the trick and all of the blood that was restricting his breathing was suddenly vomited out. A few seconds later his breathing started to return to normal, but he was still unconscious. The police and ambulance crew arrived and I left them to it and slipped away, I had blood all over me.

I disappeared into the gents' toilet. I looked down at the thick, sticky blood covering my leather gloves and sleeves of my jacket. I ran them under the cold tap and rubbed my hands together, grabbed some paper towels and wiped away the blood. The water turned red as it spiralled its way down into the waste pipe; a few minutes ago it had been quite happily pumping around inside the guy's veins. I looked at myself in the mirror and that was the moment when I decided that it was time to quit.

A punch up was one thing, but this was stupidly dangerous and unnecessary.

Ten minutes later, I went back into the bar. The blood had been mopped up, the D J had started up again and the lights had been dimmed and the punters were laughing, drinking and dancing as if nothing had happened. It was all quite surreal. I asked the lads what had happened and apparently psycho Simon had knocked the guy out and then, whilst the bloke was on his back, he smashed his face to a pulp. Those sovereign-encrusted fists had really chopped him up good style. On the scale of one to ten of stupidity, that must rate an eleven. The guy could have died, and for what? I know for a fact that we would all have gone down for that one.

EPILOGUE

I went back the next night for the last time, and that was that. I had spoken to Pete and told him that it was going to be my last night at the club. He came down later on that evening for our last nostalgic drink at the place. The music had now faded and the DJ had packed away his kit. The noisy revellers had all dispersed into the night and the club was silent and dark inside. I stepped outside into the cold, wet, deserted high street and as the bolt was drawn across the nightclub door, I stopped and took a glance back at the place for the last time. I was now just a fading memory as I walked away.

It always feels a little odd leaving a place you have worked in for years. However, to be honest I felt the timing was right, and I also felt a measure of relief in getting out of the game in one piece. Let's face it, this is a dangerous game. Imagine going to work wearing body armour and knife-proof gloves and carrying a few other 'protective items'. A mate of mine even used to bring a gum shield with him when he came to work with us. There's got to be something wrong here, and there must be an easier, better and far less hazardous way to earn a few quid.

I made my way to the car park alone and climbed into my car and sat for a moment before starting the engine. It would be ironic to get a good hiding on my last night, wouldn't it? So, not wanting to tempt fate I stayed switched on and was alert right to the end.

***

And so my journey into this strange and risky occupation has come to an end. What conclusions can I draw from the experience? I can't say that I'm proud of anything except maybe the way I handled my fears and the way that I stood up to certain individuals. All I can say is that I genuinely tried to keep the decent people safe from the drug dealers, drunks, bullies and scumbags. I took all the crap so the genuine decent punter didn't have to and that's what the job is all about.

At the beginning of the book, I asked you to stand on the door shoulder to shoulder with me. In doing so I hope I have been able to pry open the door a little to afford you a peek inside this dark, clandestine, shady world. I hope that I have given you an insight into the type of people who choose to do this thankless job, because that's the way I see it: thankless, and a job where nobody really gives a fuck about you.

To stand and face the utter dregs of society, ready to take on everything that these creatures can throw at you, night after night, is tough and it eventually takes its toll on you, no matter how strong you think you are. And given time it will damage you if you let it, so recognise the signs and go and do something else instead before it's too late. Thankfully I have now found a gentler path to follow. It's ironic though, to think that it was these very experiences that led me to the literary path.

***

I used to find it very difficult to walk away when confronted or challenged. However, my mind-set has now become somewhat more enlightened and I feel that there is no further need for me to prove myself. This way of thinking takes real strength of character, and I'm still trying hard to come to terms with the concept. It's difficult to seek another direction once you have trodden the 'warrior path' so to speak. Clichéd I know, but you catch my drift.

I have come to conclusion that to use violence as a last resort in defending oneself or in the defence of others is perfectly justifiable: anything else, however, would not be considered so. There are some karate masters, for example, whose skills have been honed to the highest levels attainable and if they were to be attacked they would only use their knowledge at the point of death, their abilities being so dangerous that, just like the deadly Japanese sword carried by the ancient samurai, they must remain sheathed. The consequences of not doing so are too terrible to comprehend.

The bouncer world became a cold, dark little realm for me, and one that in the end I was glad to leave. And I think I left just in time.

THE END

Author bio

www.billcarsonbooks.com

My first step on the rung of the literary ladder came in the form of this autobiography, which was first published in paperback in 2005. I enjoyed the writing experience so much that soon after its publication, I enrolled in an Open University fiction writing course, which, to my pleasure and amazement, I passed.

I have now written several books covering various subjects. My two crime novels, *Necessary Evils* and its sequel *Nemesis*, are my best work to date and have received some excellent reviews.

Crime fiction is something that I am passionate about. I now consider myself first and foremost to be a crime fiction writer. I am currently writing *Never Say Die*, which will be the third in the series.

Bill Carson

Glossary of Slang

Adam and Eve = believe
Acker Bilk = milk
bacon and eggs = legs
bat and wickets = tickets
battle cruiser = boozer = pub
biscuits and cheese = knees
bonce = top of the head
bottle = courage
bricks and mortar = daughter
brown bread = dead
butchers = butcher's hook = look
china plate = mate
cream-crackered = knackered
custard pie = eye
dicky bird = word
Donald Duck = luck
four by two = Jew
Fourth of July = tie
ginger ale = jail
ginger beer = queer
Gregory Peck = neck
half inch = pinch = steal
horse and cart = fart
Jack = Jack Jones = alone

Kane and Able = table
Lady Godiva = fiver
loaf of bread = head
mince pies = eyes
mud hut = gut
Nuremburg trials = piles
Pete Tong = wrong
plates of meat = feet
pork pies = lies
rabbit and pork = talk
Roman candles = sandals
rub a dub = pub
Scotch peg = leg
septic tank = yank
sky rocket = pocket
syrup of fig = wig
tea leaf = thief
Uncle Ned = bed
Vera Lynn = gin
On your uppers = the soles on your shoes have worn away leaving only the upper part exposed = devoid of cash
wallies = idiots
what's the SP? (SP = the starting prices at a race course) = what's going on?

Gallery

Printed in Great Britain
by Amazon